# ACHIEVING FINANCIAL FREEDOM

# ACHIEVING FINANCIAL FREEDOM

## Building Wealth through Passive Income in the New Digital Age of Financial Intelligence

## DR. ROBERT RAMIREZ

## DISCLAIMER

This book is for educational and informational purposes only. It is not a substitute for legal, tax, financial, or investment advice from competent professionals.

Dr. Robert Ramirez teaches wealth creation, business, and financial freedom. He does not sell, solicit, or negotiate investment vehicles and is not a financial or investment counselor. This book does not endorse any investment, security, cryptocurrency, real estate, or other investment types. Before making any major financial decision, consult a competent professional. These experts can personalize advice to your goals, experiences, and finances.

Dr. Ramirez cannot guarantee the authenticity or completeness of the information in this book, which was gathered from credible public sources. Before investing, readers should do their homework. Dr. Ramirez is not responsible for this book's faults, incompleteness, or unreliability. Any investment or substantial financial decision made based on this book's material is the reader's responsibility.

**Editing and Layout Design** by: Katherine Peterson
(https://www.fiverr.com/s/bGWZ0N)

# Dedication

I dedicate this book to the memory of my granddaughter Marlowe. She gave us the hope that her love and spirit continue to inspire us to live life with joy and strength of mind and soul. Also, to my amazing wife, Patricia, and gifted children Bryan, Michael, Melissa, Shawn, Matthew, and Megan, as well as all my grandchildren. Continue living your dreams, take on new challenges, love abundantly, and appreciate each day.

# Book Reviews

"Written for working-class folks, especially people of color and young adults struggling to pay bills and stay ahead of the bill collector, Dr. Ramirez shares how he regained his financial footing through education and sheer determination. In his book, he shares how to gain financial freedom in today's tough times while not losing your ability to love, stay healthy, and be happy. This is a must-read and profoundly timely book."

**—Dr. Gil Ontai,**
**Ed.D recipient,** Harvard Kennedy School Ash Center for Democratic Governance and Innovation.

"Dr. Ramirez's expertise and experience have given me the knowledge to properly examine my current financial status and the confidence to diversify my investments. Based on his understanding of the ever-evolving cryptocurrency market, I gained exposure to the market with a better respect for the positive potentials and awareness of its possible short-term volitivity. Dr. Ramirez started me on a path to a "Wealthy Mindset"!

**—Raymond M. Kacmar,**
Retired NASA Safety and Mission Assurance Manager

"Clear, cogent, concise, coherent practical guidance and advice is available in Dr. Ramirez's book, 'Achieving Financial Freedom.' The book is a practical, practical, ready-to-use guide for anybody wanting to gain an enhanced level of financial literacy and self-sufficiency."

**—Dr. Bob Biswas, Senior Professor,**
Business Consultant, and a former Corporate Vice President."

"This book is written for everybody aiming to enhance their financial literacy. The nexus of technology and the new economy have created challenges and opportunities that have never existed. This text provides a roadmap to help you navigate your way to financial success in this unique environment."

**—Chris Wadden,**
Chairman Emeritus Pasadena Angels

"A remarkable book for the novice and a great refresher for the veteran; building one's financial independence in the digital economy. The author(Dr. Ramirez?) generously offers a tested diversified portfolio that fits the times and demonstrates established pathways to financial freedom."

**—Moe Saouli,**
Assistant Dean, Teaching & Learning

"A learned proverb declares, 'The wealth of the rich is their fortress.' In this book, Dr. Ramirez helps us understand how to establish a personal fortress with wise words on building wealth through multiple income streams. Employing this wisdom is the key to becoming wealthy."

**—Dr. Joel W. Bunkowske,**
Esq., Professor and Attorney at Law

"Dr. Bob Ramirez's book, Achieving Financial Freedom: Building Wealth through Passive Income in the New Digital Age of Financial Intelligence, serves as a springboard from tackling household finances to becoming an investor in one's own family."

**—Marylata Elton,**
Music Producer

"Unvarying wealth management results from dignity and gratitude to others. Dr. Ramirez's authentic guidance in 'Achieving Financial Freedom' shows his commitment to learning and teaching the possibilities of building wealth through multiple income streams."

**—Dr. Paula C. Herring,**
Educator and Engagement Leader

"So much is not taught to us in our Economics classes and even in Personal Finance courses online. It's hard to trust TikTok and other social media influencers. However, Dr. Ramirez had laid out how to win with money in a short, easily consumable manner with decades of credibility behind him!"

**—William "Bill" Garrison,**
People Leader, Author, & Professor

"Wow! This is an amazing book. It was written for anyone who diligently seeks to achieve financial freedom. Dr. Ramirez has touched on all the pertinent components of what is needed to be financially stable and has written the book for the young, the old, and anyone in between. The book is written so practically that anyone can understand it and gain from its contents. Anyone seeking to understand financial literacy better should certainly read this book. "

**—Dr. Willie J. Wilborn,**
Senior Professor, Business Management Consultant, Human Resources Management Consultant, and former Associate Dean of Business and Liberal Arts Colleges.

# Contents


Book Reviews........................................................................vi

Foreword..............................................................................xi

Introduction ..................................................................... xiii

**SECTION I: THE POWER OF EDUCATION AND HOW TO GET STARTED**

Chapter 1: Richer By Education ...........................................3

Chapter 2: The TIE System..................................................22

Chapter 3: Mastering Family Finances..............................25

**SECTION II: DEVELOPING YOUR STREAMS OF INCOME**

Chapter 4: Multiplied Wealth ............................................33

Chapter 5: Why Settle for One? .......................................36

**SECTION III: GET STARTED WITH TRADING STOCKS**

Chapter 6: Stock Market 101..............................................71

Chapter 7: Financial Statements that Matter ................106

Chapter 8: Economic Indicators for Smart Investing ..............126

Chapter 9: Monetary vs. Fiscal Policy..............................128

Chapter 10: Gold, Silver, and Beyond..............................135

Chapter 11: Real Estate Riches .........................................144

Chapter 12: Side Hustles and Entrepreneurship ........................163

Chapter 13: Debt Management and Credit Mastery..................191

Chapter 14: The Digital Frontier .....................................206


## SECTION IV: PLANNING FOR YOUR FUTURE


Chapter 15: The Future of Social Security....................235

Chapter 16: Financial Planning for The Future.........................243


## SECTION V: PULLING IT ALL TOGETHER


Chapter 17: Financial Freedom Strategy.....................................247

Recommended Reading ...............................................255

References..................................................................261

# Foreword by Michael Gary Milford

I was honored when Dr. Robert Ramirez reached out to me to write the foreword to his book "Achieving Financial Freedom". We have been colleagues at the same university for fourteen years. Dr. Ramirez considers me a close friend and mentor. With extensive experience with business start-ups and turnarounds with high-tech companies and private career schools, Robert felt I would be the right person to write the foreword to his book.

Over the years Robert has shared his passion for achieving financial freedom with his students. His approach is simple, direct, and practical.

Three things I want you to know about this book:

1.  It is an empowering guide to achieving financial freedom in today's fast-paced, technology-driven world.

2.  This book is a must-read for anyone who wants to learn how to build wealth through multiple income streams.

3.  With his practical insights and step-by-step guidance, Dr. Ramirez takes readers on a journey toward financial success.

Two things I want you to know more about from this book:

1.  How to build wealth through "passive" income in the new digital age of Financial Intelligence.

2.  The importance of diversifying your income streams.

One key takeaway from this book:

The importance of diversifying your income streams. In the digital age, there are countless opportunities to earn money online, and Dr. Ramirez provides a roadmap for identifying and capitalizing on these opportunities. Whether you want to start a side hustle or build a full-time business, this book offers valuable insights on achieving financial independence.

With extensive business and new market development knowledge and having taught multiple graduate courses in entrepreneurship, I believe Dr. Ramirez's expertise and guidance will empower readers to take control of their finances and build the wealth they deserve. Whether you're a seasoned investor or just starting, this book is a valuable resource for anyone looking to succeed in the new digital age.

# Introduction

The whole world waited with bated breath as Dr. Doom, the nickname for economist Nouriel Roubini, came out of the shadows and made a terrifying prediction (Stokes 2021). His dire warning sent shockwaves through the financial markets and shook our society to its very core. The words "stagflationary bust" hung in the air like a death sentence, threatening to throw us all back into darkness.

Memories of the global financial crisis that Dr. Doom had predicted in 2008 were still fresh in the minds of those that didn't survive it, and the mere mention of another economic meltdown sent waves of anxiety rippling across the globe (Garcia 2022). The cuts and scars were still raw, and the wounds were still open. Even the bravest of us got shivers when we heard someone talk about another economic meltdown (Stokes 2021). The future looked scary and uncertain, and the livelihoods of millions of people were in danger (Garcia 2022). As families got ready for what was coming, the disaster that was about to happen pressed down on us all, as the world economy felt like it was about to fall apart again, the only certain thing was that we had a long and hard road ahead of us.

The future is still unclear, and the problems that lay ahead can be scary. However, when bad things happen, we can stay strong and we can ready ourselves for whatever the world has in store ahead for us. Through learning about financial intelligence, and building wealth through multiple income streams, we cannot only overcome the challenges that come our way but also create a better future for our families. By understanding how money works and making smart financial decisions, we can build a solid foundation of financial stability and security for ourselves and our loved ones. So let us embrace the power of financial education and take control of our financial future, paving the way for a brighter and more prosperous tomorrow.

For a lot of people, the recession meant more than just losing their jobs and having banks close. It meant losing their homes and dreams and having a hard time for the rest of their lives. The future looked darker, and financial insecurities left holes where hope once was. Businesses, too, were hit hard by the recession. Companies that had been thriving just months before suddenly struggled to stay afloat as the economy crumbled around them. Retail stores closed their doors, factories shut down, and entire industries came to a grinding halt, leaving countless workers without jobs and families without income.

The effects of the recession were felt far and wide as people from all walks of life struggled to survive. Families had to make tough decisions, like either paying their mortgage or putting food on the table. Children went without necessities like clothing and school supplies, as their parents struggled to make ends meet.

I was one of the many people who were hit hard by the recession, which led to the loss of my job and the sale of my family house. I worked as the Director of Information Technology for over 18 years and built a successful career for myself. I had a beautiful home where my wife and I raised our six kids and planted several plants and trees in the yard. Life was good, and I was proud of everything we had accomplished.

But when the recession hit, everything changed. My employer got hit hard and moved to another state while laying off a significant portion of their workforce, including me. Suddenly, I found myself without a job, struggling to find work in a market where opportunities were scarce. As the months passed, it became clear that I could not keep up with my mortgage payments. I had no choice but to put my family home up for sale, a house that was filled with memories and had been a sanctuary for my family.

The process of selling our home was painful. Every brick and tree in the yard we had carefully tended would be left behind. The walls that had witnessed many milestones in our family's life had to be stripped bare. As each item was packed up and taken away, it felt like we were losing a part of ourselves. Despite the heartache and stress, I never lost hope. I knew our family and I would get through this difficult time. We had each other, and that was all that mattered.

Today, I am grateful for the lessons I learned during that challenging time. The experience taught me the value of resilience, perseverance, and the importance of family. Although I lost my job and had to sell my family home was a wake-up call for me. I gained a newfound appreciation of what truly matters in life: love, health, and happiness. It made me realize that relying on a single source of income was a risky strategy, especially during difficult times like the 2008 recession. I learned that having multiple income streams was essential to building financial stability and resilience. I began exploring different ways to earn additional income. I started a side business, offering small businesses IT and consulting services. It was challenging and required a lot of hard work, but also incredibly rewarding. I was able to use my skills and experience to help other entrepreneurs succeed while also generating additional income for myself and my family. I also began investing in stocks and other assets, looking for opportunities to earn passive income. I learned about different investment strategies and how to manage risk effectively. Over time, these investments began to generate income for me, providing a buffer against the ups and downs of the economy.

I didn't stop there. I made it my mission to help others learn about the importance of multiple income streams. I started sharing my experience and knowledge with my students, friends, family, and acquaintances, and soon, I found that I had a passion for educating others.

As an author, business professor, and investor, I've spent many years giving people the tools they need to build their money streams and become financially independent. I've helped a lot of students get better at Financial Intelligence over the years, and I continue to do so every day. With my help, you can get the same financial security and independence that I've won through hard work and commitment. And, as I show in this book, that's not the end of the road to success. I've also pushed myself to new heights by getting a Doctor of Business Administration in International Business and an Advanced Certificate in Blockchain and Digital Assets as well as numerous courses on stock investing. Let me show you how to make your personal and business dreams come true. It's my way of giving back and assisting others in achieving the same financial stability and resilience that I have gained and learned the hard way.

# SECTION I:
# THE POWER OF EDUCATION AND
# HOW TO GET STARTED

# CHAPTER 1: RICHER BY EDUCATION

## HARNESSING THE POWER OF LEARNING TO BUILD WEALTH

---

"The only person you are destined to become is the person you decide to be."—**Ralph Waldo Emerson**

---

*Keep your beliefs pure and good because ...*
*Your beliefs become your thoughts;*
*Your thoughts become your words;*
*Your words become your actions;*
*Your actions become your habits;*
*Your habits become your values;*
*Your values become your destiny.*

—**Mahatma Gandhi**

I stood at the classroom podium, my eyes' piercing gaze scanning the sea of eager students before me. It was the first day of class, and the air was thick with anticipation as the class leaned forward, waiting for me to speak. I took a deep breath, my eyes narrowing with determination.

"Welcome," my voice booming through the class. "I am Dr. Bob Ramirez, and I am here to talk to you today about a subject crucial to your success in this new digital age—Financial Intelligence." The classroom fell silent as I spoke, my words ringing out with a force that demanded attention from my experience with rebuilding my financial stability.

"Many of you are here today because you want to learn how to build wealth," I continued. "You want to know the secrets of those who have made it to the top and have achieved financial freedom and independence. And I am here to tell you that the key to that success lies in your ability to generate multiple income streams." There was a murmur of agreement from the students, and I nodded, my eyes sparkling with intensity to help yet another class of students.

"In this new digital age, the game's rules have changed; the old ways of doing things no longer work. You must adapt, evolve, and learn new skills and strategies to succeed." I could see that my students hung on this every word, their eyes wide with a hunger for knowledge. "And that is why I am here," I said. "To help you develop the financial intelligence, you need to thrive in this new world. To show you how to build wealth through multiple streams of income. To give you the tools and the knowledge to take control of your financial future."

There was a pause. I leaned forward, dropping my voice to a low, intense whisper. "Are you ready?" I asked. "Are you ready to take the first step on this journey? To embrace the power of financial intelligence and to use it to create the life of your dreams?" The room was filled with excitement. I smiled confidently, eager to get started. "Let's begin," I said. "We'll work together to build our wealth and create our future."

Welcome class let's start with Achieving Financial Freedom: Building Wealth through Passive Income in the New Digital Age of Financial Intelligence. I'm Dr. Bob Ramirez, a Business and Entrepreneur professor, and investor, who will move you forward on your journey toward enlightened financial education and financial freedom. Did you know that the average millionaire has several streams of income?

## My Early Thoughts About Learning Related to Money

My parents taught me the value of working hard and saving a dollar. My mom would hide her extra money in foil paper in the freezer until she had enough cash to buy us something special. She did not drive, so we walked everywhere, sometimes hauling our little red wagon full of groceries. As a child, I learned how to start saving from the time I had my first paper route at nine years old.

My mom was a great, loving, and giving parent I loved and respected. My dad, always working, was an excellent provider for our family of seven. After serving in the military, he worked his entire life as a railroad locomotive electrician, working long hours to keep the trains moving. In addition, he worked overtime to pay for our private schools and keep a roof over our heads. He was a strict disciplinarian who you did not want to disappoint. Being untruthful was never tolerated; his large green eyes would pierce my inner core. My parents taught me great lifelong lessons at a young age which included respect, honesty, working hard, and perseverance.

My mom came from a family of thirteen in Jalisco, Mexico, and had to quit school early to care for her sibling on the ranch. Unfortunately, my mom only had a third-grade education. My parents taught me to save but not how to invest and grow my money. In grade school, I was not as bright as the others. I would hide behind other students, so my teacher would not call on me to read or spell in front of my peers. I could do math but was behind in my English and spelling skills. However, at a very early stage, I learned I could outwork others and kept my learning momentum moving forward, becoming a Doctor of Business (DBA) and a University professor.

---

"I'm not a genius. I'm just a tremendous bundle of experience." —**R. Buckminster Fuller**

---

## Start With a Positive Wealthy Mindset

A wealthy mindset is about more than just having a lot of money. It's a mindset focused on gratitude, abundance, opportunity, and possibility. When you have a wealthy mindset, you approach life with an optimistic outlook and are open to the many opportunities that come your way.

A key attribute of a prosperous mindset is its emphasis on abundance. Rather than adopting a mentality of scarcity, which revolves around beliefs such as "resources are limited," a wealthy mindset centers on abundance and fosters thoughts like "resources are abundant, and I can access my share of them." This abundance-focused outlook opens up a realm of opportunities and possibilities, as it does not restrict individuals with limiting thoughts of scarcity.

Another important aspect of a wealthy mindset is a focus on

opportunity. When you have a wealthy mindset, you are always looking for opportunities to grow, learn, and improve yourself. You are not afraid to take risks and look for new and exciting opportunities to help you achieve your goals.

A wealthy mindset also involves a strong sense of self-belief and confidence. When you believe in yourself and your abilities, you are more likely to take risks, try new things, and pursue your goals passionately and enthusiastically. This self-belief also helps you to overcome obstacles and challenges, as you can maintain an optimistic outlook even in the face of adversity.

Finally, a wealthy mindset focuses on the bigger picture. Instead of being bogged down by life's day-to-day challenges and stresses, a wealthy mindset is focused on the long term, with a clear vision of where you want to go and what you want to achieve. This big-picture thinking helps you to stay motivated and focused even when the going gets tough. It's important to set your mind to focus on abundance, opportunity, self-belief, and big-picture thinking. By adopting this mindset, you can achieve your goals, overcome challenges, and create a life full of joy, satisfaction, and success.

Wealth building and financial education were not taught in our schools and certainly not discussed at the dinner table by my parents. In our society, you never wanted to talk about money or lack of funds, but you were always taught to be grateful for what you had. My parents were very religious, and the church was a foundation in my early years. Religion made me feel better about myself and made me part of a larger culture. Being an altar boy gave me responsibility and higher self-esteem. Our family donated each week to help the church and families in need. I learned early the good feeling of helping others, which developed the idea of financial wealth enlightenment, strengthening our society. Talking about money and politics at the family's dinner table was discouraged back then. There was little open-minded discussion or consideration for another point of view.

## Consider Yourself Rich

My friend John was born into a middle-class family in the heart of America. His hard-working and dedicated parents instilled in him the value of persistence and self-reliance. From a young age, John knew that success was not just a dream but a tangible goal that could be achieved through hard work, determination, and following his dreams and passions.

As he grew up, John excelled in school and pursued his education with a singular focus. He earned a degree in business and started working in finance, quickly climbing the ranks to become a top executive at a large corporation. With his talent for numbers and strategic thinking, John amassed a fortune that allowed him to live a life of luxury and privilege.

But wealth was not just about material possessions or financial security for John. It was about providing for his family, ensuring their health and happiness, and building a legacy that would endure for generations. He poured his heart and soul into his work but never lost sight of the things that truly mattered.

Despite his success, John faced his fair share of challenges. He weathered the storms of economic downturns and market fluctuations, constantly adapting and innovating to stay ahead of the curve. And when his health worsened, he faced it head-on, never losing his fighting spirit or his will to succeed. Through it all, John remained a family man at heart. He doted on his children, taking them on exotic vacations and showering them with gifts. And when his wife fell ill, he was there for her every step of the way, providing the love and support she needed to recover.

In the end, John's success resulted from his American dream and hard work, dedication, and unwavering spirit. He had achieved the ultimate goal of the American dream: to provide for his family and leave a lasting legacy that would endure for generations. And in the process, he became a true hero in the eyes of those he loved and inspired.

You are already wealthy in many more ways than you can imagine. Let me list just a few. How many of these do you already possess?

- You are living the American dream with the bountiful opportunities the United States provides.

- Sharing life with a significant other brings the loving closeness of wealth to the fullness of life, which is true richness.

- You have children that you lovingly raise and who will be your legacy.

- Your friendships with colleagues, family, and school friends are your bank of riches.

- Your community and home are contributions to fairness and equality.

- Your freedom and independence allow enlightened wealth and opportunities.

- Your ability to continue your education and learn new skills.

- Your health and wellness, as stores of strength for your body, mind, and spirit.

In a purely material sense, all the assets in your possession constitute your wealth. Your net worth is the most typical way to demonstrate wealth financially. Money is the most popular way to measure wealth in today's culture, however, your legacy will be one of character, the richness of family, fulfillment, wellness of spirit, and strong honest relationships.

## The current state of money and finance in America

The state of money and finance in America currently is one of financial anxiety, with many Americans struggling to keep up with rising costs and inflation. Housing prices have continued to rise, making it difficult for many Americans to afford a home, while the cost of utilities and gasoline have also increased. At the same time, the savings rate of Americans remains low, leaving many vulnerable to financial shocks.

One of the most pressing issues facing Americans is the rising cost of housing. Housing prices have increased significantly over the past many years, driven by low-interest rates and a shortage of homes for sale. This has made it difficult for many Americans to purchase a home, particularly in high-demand areas. As a result, many are forced to rent, which can be an expensive option.

In addition to the high housing cost, Americans face rising utility costs. The cost of electricity and gas has increased in recent years, making it more expensive to heat and cool homes. This can be particularly challenging for those living on a fixed income or with low wages, who may struggle to pay their bills.

Another significant challenge facing Americans is the rising cost of gasoline. The price of gasoline has increased significantly in recent years, driven by a combination of factors, including rising demand and geopolitical tensions. This has made it more expensive to travel, particularly for those who rely on their vehicles for work or other essential activities.

All these factors contribute to a general sense of financial anxiety among Americans. In addition to these specific challenges, many are concerned about the overall state of the economy and the potential for another recession. This can make it challenging to plan for the future, particularly for those living paycheck to paycheck.

Compounding these challenges is the issue of inflation. Inflation has been rising in recent years, driven by supply chain disruptions and increased demand for goods and services. This has increased prices for many everyday items, including food, clothing, and household goods. The increased cost of necessities can be particularly challenging for those on a fixed income or with low wages, as they may struggle to afford them.

Finally, the savings rate of Americans remains low. Many live paychecks to paycheck, with little or no savings to fall back on during an emergency. This can make weathering financial shocks, such as job loss or unexpected medical expenses difficult.

So here we are, the current state of money and finance in America is one of financial anxiety. Americans are facing rising housing prices, utility costs, gasoline prices, inflation, and low savings rates. These challenges contribute to a general sense of insecurity and uncertainty, making it difficult for many to plan for the future. Policymakers and financial institutions need to take these challenges seriously and work to find solutions that can help Americans manage their finances more effectively.

Financial anxiety is a pervasive issue affecting more than three-quarters of the population, with over 77% of individuals grappling with it. With escalating costs of housing, utilities, gasoline, bills, and taxes, coupled with the unpredictable nature of the economy, it's no wonder that people are feeling the pinch. Although interest rates have risen by twofold since 2022, they are still historically low, which presents both a challenge and an opportunity for individuals looking to secure their financial future.

## Financial illiteracy in America

Building financial literacy in America is a major issue that affects individuals and society at large. It refers to the lack of understanding of basic economic concepts such as budgeting, saving, investing, and debt management. Unfortunately, this crucial subject is not taught in most schools in the United States, which has contributed to the widening wealth gap in the country.

The wealth gap in the United States has been increasing for decades, with the top 1% of households owning more wealth than the bottom 90% combined. While various factors contribute to this trend, financial illiteracy is a significant driver. Financially literate people are better equipped to manage their money, invest wisely, and make informed financial decisions that can help them build wealth over time.

Without a strong foundation in financial literacy, many people fall victim to predatory financial practices, such as high-interest loans, payday lending, and credit card debt. These practices can quickly erode a person's financial well-being, making it difficult to save or invest for the future.

Furthermore, schools' lack of financial education perpetuates a cycle of poverty, where disadvantaged communities are more likely to suffer from financial illiteracy. In many cases, children from low-income families do not have access to the same financial resources and education as their more affluent peers, making it even harder for them to overcome financial hurdles later in life.

To address this issue, it is crucial to prioritize financial literacy in our schools. Financial education should be incorporated into the curriculum early, starting with basic money management skills and building up to more advanced concepts. Students should learn about budgeting, saving, investing, debt management, and credit scores, among other topics.

By equipping students with the knowledge and tools to make informed financial decisions, we can help bridge the wealth gap in our country. Financial literacy is essential for individual success and the prosperity of our society as a whole. It is time for our educational institutions to recognize the importance of financial education and take action to ensure that every student has access to this vital subject.

Financial illiteracy is a significant driver of America's wealth gap. 90 % of high school graduates are financially illiterate. According to a study conducted by the American Payroll Association in 2021, approximately 59% of Americans report living from paycheck to paycheck (APA, 2021). It's time to start teaching people how to build multiple forms of wealth. Here are some additional concerning statistics from the "Report on the Economic Well-Being of U.S.

Households in 2020" (Board of Governors of the Federal Reserve System, 2021): Statistics from the "Report on the Economic Well-Being of U.S. Households in 2020" (Board of Governors of the Federal Reserve System, 2021):

- 39% of Americans would not be able to cover a $400 emergency expense without borrowing money or selling assets. (p. 6)

- 22% of adults experienced a major unexpected medical expense in 2020. (p. 8)

- 36% of adults who were employed in February 2020 and were laid off during the pandemic were not employed in January 2021. (p. 12)

- 25% of adults who were not retired and were not working in January 2021 cited COVID-19 as the main reason for not working. (p. 12)

- 13% of adults with a mortgage or rent payment were not caught up on payments in January 2021. (p. 14)

- 44% of adults who did not have a bachelor's degree reported that they would struggle to pay for an unexpected $400 expense, compared to 18% of adults with a bachelor's degree or higher. (p. 17)

- 28% of adults who had not graduated from high school reported that they would struggle to pay for an unexpected $400 expense. (p. 17)

- 40% of adults with a household income below $40,000 reported that they would struggle to pay for an unexpected $400 expense, compared to 17% of adults with a household income above

$40,000. (p. 18)

According to research from fools.com, the average American's savings is only $3,500. Moreover, 29% of Americans don't even have a saving account. As I write this book, 401(K) accounts are crashing, and pensions are being gutted. So, taking charge of your investments, financial future, and retirement would be best. Investing in your financial education will multiply your knowledge and money.

What would happen if you put $1 into an investment for 30 years? You wouldn't miss $1 every day or much money, but you'd be surprised at how much $1 would grow to over 30 years if it were invested. If you were to invest $1 every day into an investment that compounds annually at a rate of 10% for 30 years, you would see a significant increase in your investment.

Assuming that you invest every day for 30 years, you would be making a total of 30 x 365 = 10,950 investments. At the end of the first year, your initial investment of $365 would grow to $401.50, with a return of $36.50. In the second year, the interest would be calculated based on the new balance of $401.50, resulting in a return of $41.65, and a new balance of $443.15.

This compounding effect continues for 30 years, with your investment growing exponentially each year. After 30 years, your total investment of $10,950 would grow to approximately $175,712.22, with a return of $164,762.22.

It's important to note that this is assuming an annual compounding rate of 10%. If the investment is compounded more frequently, such as daily or monthly, the returns would be even greater due to the effect of compounding. However, keep in mind that all investments carry some level of risk, and historical performance is not a guarantee of future results. Additionally, it's important to consider the impact of inflation and taxes on your investment returns.

## Successful Entrepreneurs

It's important to note that the world's most successful entrepreneurs, investors, and business owners had to start somewhere. They bring a passion for doing what they love, building something, and adding value to a service or product. For example, Jeff Bezos worked out of his garage in Seattle, Washington, and started Amazon as an online bookstore with several employees. He started Amazon in 1994 using some borrowed money from his parents and others. As of 2022, Amazon has a market capitalization of 1.3 trillion dollars and is the second largest company in the world behind Walmart. In 2004, Mark Zuckerberg created and started a new website called Facebook. He named the site after the student directories handed out to Harvard University students to help them get to know one another better, then progressed to expand to millions of faces adding value along the way. He started Facebook at 19 years old in his Harvard dorm room, and it is now worth about 57 billion dollars.

The benefits of multiple forms of income, owning a business, and investing are far too great to pass up. Whether you're looking to create passive income, save for retirement, or build generational wealth, investing is the best way to ensure you reach your financial goals. In this book, as a professor, I will guide and educate you about the most proven methods of multiple income streams.

I wanted to inspire you with this message. Philosopher Sir Francis Bacon, back in the 1780s, said, "Knowledge is power." So true! Knowledge is power, but only when you know how to use it. Through education, you gain knowledge, understanding, and wisdom. Knowledge is information. Understanding is comprehending that information, and wisdom is knowing how to apply helpful information. Wisdom is what I want for you!

You, too, can learn how to compound your wealth with financial education. First, you will build a skill set no one can take away from you. Skills that you can use will grow each week in your financial journey toward financial freedom. Your brain primarily consists of billions of neurons, more than all the stars you can see. Your neurons are cells that act as a messenger, sending information as nerve impulses (like electrical signals) to other neurons. By feeding your brain with education, you can create more neurons. This phenomenon is called neuroplasticity, which is the ability of your brain to grow, change, and strengthen. These electronic connections get stronger the more you read, study, and practice. The messages (nerve impulses) are transmitted faster and more efficiently as your links get stronger. It is how you advance in anything you study, whether it is chess, reading, money, or sports. Then, apply the knowledge and experience, with integrity and good character, to create your brand of intelligent wealth.

## The Pain of the Great Recession

The Great Recession of 2008–2009 was a dark period in global economic history that caused widespread pain and suffering for millions. It was a perfect storm of factors, including the housing market crash, widespread sub-prime lending, and the collapse of several major financial institutions that led to the most severe economic downturn since the Great Depression.

The Great Recession had far-reaching effects on the average person.

Many lost their jobs and struggled to make ends meet, while others saw their retirement savings evaporate. The impact on the housing market was particularly severe as home values plummeted, and many homeowners found themselves with mortgages worth more than their homes.

One of the primary causes of the Great Recession was the widespread practice of sub-prime lending. Banks were loaning money to people with poor credit histories, allowing them to purchase homes they could not afford. When the housing bubble burst, many borrowers could not pay their mortgages, and banks were left with massive foreclosures.

Another contributing factor was the collapse of several major financial institutions, including Lehman Brothers and Bear Stearns. This caused a crisis of confidence in the banking system, as people worried that their deposits might not be safe. This led to bank failures and forced the government to take unprecedented steps to shore up the financial system.

The effects of the Great Recession were devastating for many people. Unemployment soared, reaching double digits in some areas, and it took years for the job market to recover. Many people lost their homes, and their retirement savings declined sharply. The impact on mental health was also significant, as people struggled with anxiety, depression, and other mental health issues related to the financial stress of the time. While the economy has recovered, the scars of the Great Recession still linger for many who experienced its pain firsthand.

I was one of those who lost their job. I also had real estate tenants who were not paying me because they had lost their jobs. I had to sell our large house quickly because I knew I could not continue to pay the mortgage without a good-paying job. I was quickly depleting our savings reserves. At the time, companies were not expanding; instead, they were laying off employees in droves. I had to move my entire family from the house where we invested so much love. It was a difficult time for my family. I vowed to fix it and become more robust and financially secure, accelerating my financial education and moving toward financial freedom.

Tony Robins, bestselling author, and business strategist say, "Whatever you focus on, you're going to feel. Focus = Feeling. So, if you let someone else take control of your focus, your life will be in someone else's hand, but if you take control of your focus, you take control of your life." I began to focus on financial freedom.

## To Your Success

In this environment that we are currently in, we are faced with many problems. We will not focus on our day's global and economic issues but on what we can control. To be successful, we must motivate ourselves to keep moving forward. Make good choices and turn them into good daily habits; you won't regret them.

1. Constantly grow and improve your knowledge of building multiple streams of income.

2. Use the resources in this book to get started and continue your financial education.

3. Have a strong mindset focused on positivity, growth, learning, and achievement.

4. Give gratitude daily for the wealth and gifts you already have.

## A Systemic System for Learning

I had always dreamed of achieving financial independence. I wanted to live on my terms and not be held back by financial constraints. But I knew it wouldn't be easy. It would take a well-thought-out plan and a lot of hard work.

Fortunately, I had a secret weapon: a system of time, education, and investments I had developed over the years. It was a complex web of strategies and tactics designed to move me toward my goal of financial independence.

At its core, the system was based on time and education. I knew I needed to invest my time wisely to achieve my goal. I also knew I must continually educate myself about the markets and the economy to make intelligent investment decisions.

My system was not for the faint of heart. It required discipline, focus, and a willingness to take risks. But I was up for the challenge. I started by setting aside a portion of my monthly income for investments. I carefully researched different types of investments and diversified my portfolio to minimize risk. I also monitored the markets closely, adjusting my portfolio as needed. But I knew that investments alone would not be enough. I needed to earn more income if I wanted to achieve financial independence. So, I also focused on my education and skills. I took online courses and attended seminars to learn more about finance, entrepreneurship, and marketing. I also started a side business to generate additional income. And I made sure to network with other successful businesspeople, learning from their experiences and insights.

Over time, my system began to pay off. The investments grew, and my business became more successful. I was able to pay off many debts and build up a nest egg for the future. And as my income grew, I was able to invest even more.

Eventually, I started to achieve my goal of financial independence. I will be looking to retire soon, travel the world with my wife, and live life on my terms. And I knew it was all thanks to my time, education, and investment system.

This book will explore and teach how to build multiple income streams and combine them with my "TIE" method. Think about the first time you tied your shoe or put a tie around your neck. It wasn't visually clear or easy to do without the proper guidance or instructions. It also took practice, but soon, you were tying your shoes or neckties with little effort. There is no one correct answer for everyone, so we have to have multiple income streams. Everyone is different, and everyone has different goals and risk tolerances. What may work for you may not be the right answer for someone else.

# CHAPTER 2: THE TIE SYSTEM

## A COMPREHENSIVE GUIDE TO INVESTING FOR FINANCIAL SUCCESS

> "The stock market is filled with individuals who know the price of everything but the value of nothing."
> —Phillip Fisher

The TIE system is a powerful approach to achieving financial independence that revolves around three key components: Time, Investments, and Education. Individuals can create a solid foundation for long-term financial success by combining these three elements.

The first component of the TIE system is time. This refers to the importance of starting early and allowing investments to compound over time. By giving investments time to grow, individuals can benefit from the power of compound interest, which can significantly increase the value of their investments.

The second component of the TIE system is Investments. This refers to the importance of making intelligent investment decisions and building a diversified portfolio that includes a range of assets, such as stocks, bonds, and real estate. Individuals can grow wealth by investing wisely and creating a more secure financial future.

The final component of the TIE system is education. This refers to the importance of learning about personal finance and investing and staying informed about changes in the market and economic conditions. Individuals can make informed decisions and take control of their financial future by continually educating themselves about financial matters.

Overall, the TIE system is a comprehensive approach to achieving financial independence that emphasizes the importance of time, investments, and education. By following these principles, individuals can build a solid foundation for long-term financial success and achieve their goals.

The TIE is a mnemonic acronym that I define as Time, Investments, and Education, when tied together, will move you toward Financial Independence. Figure 1.0 below shows the TIE system working together to create financial independence..

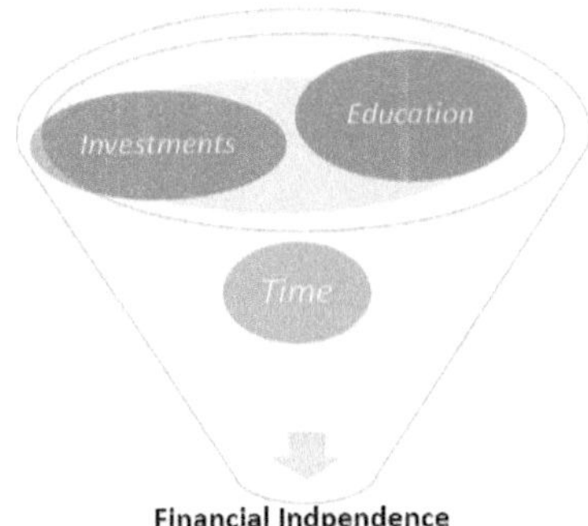


*Figure 1.0: View of the Financial Independence Funnel*

Here are just a few of the topics you will learn about:

- What are the best types of investments in today's environment?
- Financial Statements and Financial ratios that matter
- Managing your own money in the stock market
- Fix your credit report and save thousands
- Build your own business by starting with a side hustle
- Monetary vs. Fiscal Policy
- The most important Economic Indicators to follow
- Crypto Assets and the Future of Investing
- The Future of Social Security

# CHAPTER 3: MASTERING FAMILY FINANCES

## A PRACTICAL GUIDE
## TO BUILDING WEALTH

"Money is usually attracted, not pursued." —**Jim Rohn**

Managing your family finances effectively is one of the most important things you can do to ensure a stable and prosperous future. Like a successful business, managing family finances requires careful planning, strategic thinking, and clear goals and objectives. By making your family finances your number one business priority, you can set yourself up for success and achieve your financial goals.

The first step in managing your family finances like a business is to define your mission statement. This statement should clearly state your family's financial goals and why they are important. This could include saving for your children's education, paying off debt, or building an emergency fund. Having a clear mission statement lets you focus on your financial goals and make decisions that align with your family's overall financial vision.

The next step is to define your vision statement, which outlines the long-term financial goals you hope to achieve. The financial goals could include retiring comfortably, buying a home, or starting a business. Your vision statement should inspire and motivate, remind you of the bigger picture, and help you focus on your financial goals.

Once you have your mission and vision statements, it's time to develop a strategy for achieving your goals. The strategy might include creating a budget, investing in a retirement plan, or cutting back on expenses. Your design should be flexible enough to adapt to changing circumstances but focused enough to keep you on track to your long-term financial goals.

Finally, setting specific goals and objectives is important to help you measure your progress and stay motivated. These could include saving a certain amount of money each month, paying off a specific debt, or investing in a particular type of asset. You can track your progress and celebrate your successes by setting clear goals.

Making your family finances your top business priority can help you achieve financial success and stability. By defining your mission and vision statements, developing a strategic plan, and setting specific goals and objectives, you can create a roadmap for your family's financial future. With dedication, hard work, and a clear vision, you can realize your financial dreams and enjoy the benefits of financial freedom and security. Like any business, you must include the following steps to communicate your purpose.

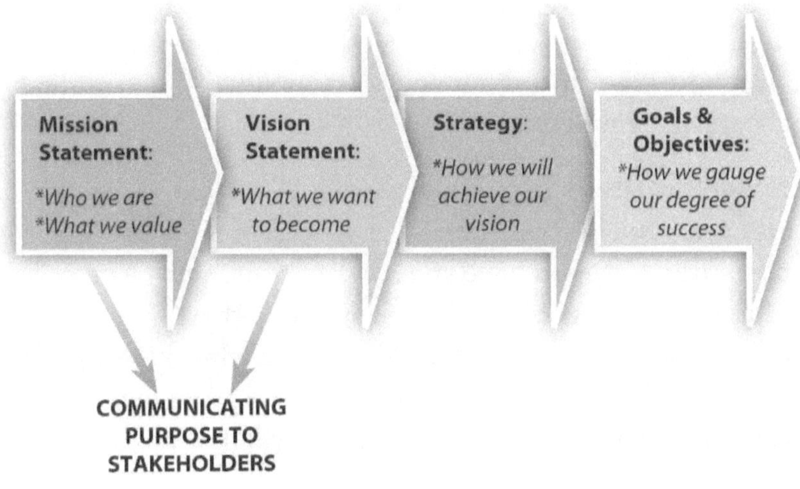


*Figure 3: communicating your purpose steps*

"The way of success is the way of the continuous pursuit of knowledge." —**Napoleon Hill**

- Create a positive and wealthy mindset

- Let's figure out your starting point. Create your personal budget and net worth statement.

- Start with paying off your high-interest credit cards

- Save 3–6 months emergency fund cash reserve that's specifically set aside for unplanned expenses or financial emergencies

- Start investing

## How Much Should I Be Saving

You want to save between 10% and 15% of your income. American savers aren't the finest in the world, let's face it. Evidently, we think that the sun will always shine, therefore we don't need to worry about having a "rainy day" fund. Nothing is more false than it is. Biblical advice on saving money protects us from harm during uncertain economic times.

Planning is what we mean when we talk about saving money. Yet in order to plan, you must become serious about your finances. Control over what you have and want to save must be exercised. You can be on the right track, but if you just sit there, you might get run over, as someone once stated. You are undoubtedly "on the right track" once you make a commitment to start saving money. But if it is only a plan that is never carried out, it will never be successful.

When you do start a savings strategy, you'll frequently run against roadblocks along the way. Keep in mind that there are plenty of alluring parking spots along the path to success. There will always be something that will conflict with your saving strategy. Thus, I advocate automating your savings plan. With direct deposit and the automatic debiting of predetermined portions of your paycheck into your savings account, this is now readily performed.

Maybe some of you already have a planned savings strategy. Great! Others may find it challenging to develop the habit of routinely conserving money. This is particularly true if you are currently barely scraping by without saving money. If this applies to you, one of the most important financial actions you can make right now is to establish a systematic savings program.

## Your Saving Accounts

The interest rates for savings accounts can vary depending on the financial institution and the type of account. Generally, online banks and credit unions offer higher interest rates than traditional brick-and-mortar banks.

As of May 2023, the highest interest rates for online savings accounts are around 3.5% to 5.00% APY (annual percentage yield). However, it's important to note that interest rates can frequently change, so it's important to compare rates regularly and check for any updates from your financial institution.

Additionally, some financial institutions may offer promotional rates or bonus offers for opening a new savings account or meeting certain requirements, such as maintaining a minimum balance or making a certain number of deposits.

When looking for the best rates for a savings account, it's important to consider other factors, such as account fees, minimum balance requirements, and account features. Choosing a savings account that fits your financial needs and goals is important, rather than just focusing on the interest rate alone.

## Steps to Building Your Wealth

For those of you who are serious about creating multiple streams of income, here's the secret that the wealthy have used for centuries:

- Develop a sizeable cash flow from several passive income streams.

- Use the cash flow as investment capital for investing in appreciating assets, like real estate, to provide even more cash flow and tax benefits.

- Repeat.

It sounds easy, doesn't it? Well, it's not. Simple, yes. Easy, no. There's a big difference. While this is the secret recipe for creating massive wealth, it will take hard work, dedication, and commitment. It will mean sacrificing some television time and other leisure activities.

I always tell my student to focus on adding value. If your goal is to create wealth, you must focus on value creation. With value creation comes wealth. Did you know that almost all income streams come from these three sources?

- Real Estate
- Paper and digital assets
- A business or side hustle

## The Importance of Creating Multiple Income Streams

The secret to achieving financial freedom should not be a mystery. It is a very straightforward process that anyone can apply if they have the proper knowledge, a positive attitude, and a burning passion for success. Since 2011, I have been on a mission to help my students move towards financial freedom. These students come from all walks of life and understand the importance of wise financial management. Three basic principles of creating multiple income streams lay at the core of my financial teaching.

In today's challenging economy, developing multiple income streams from different sources is more important than ever. Never in our country have so many Americans been one paycheck away from bankruptcy or foreclosure on their homes.

1. Create a sizeable amount of cash flow
2. Invest the cash flow into appreciating assets for more cash flow and tax benefits
3. Repeat

# SECTION II:
# DEVELOPING YOUR STREAMS OF INCOME

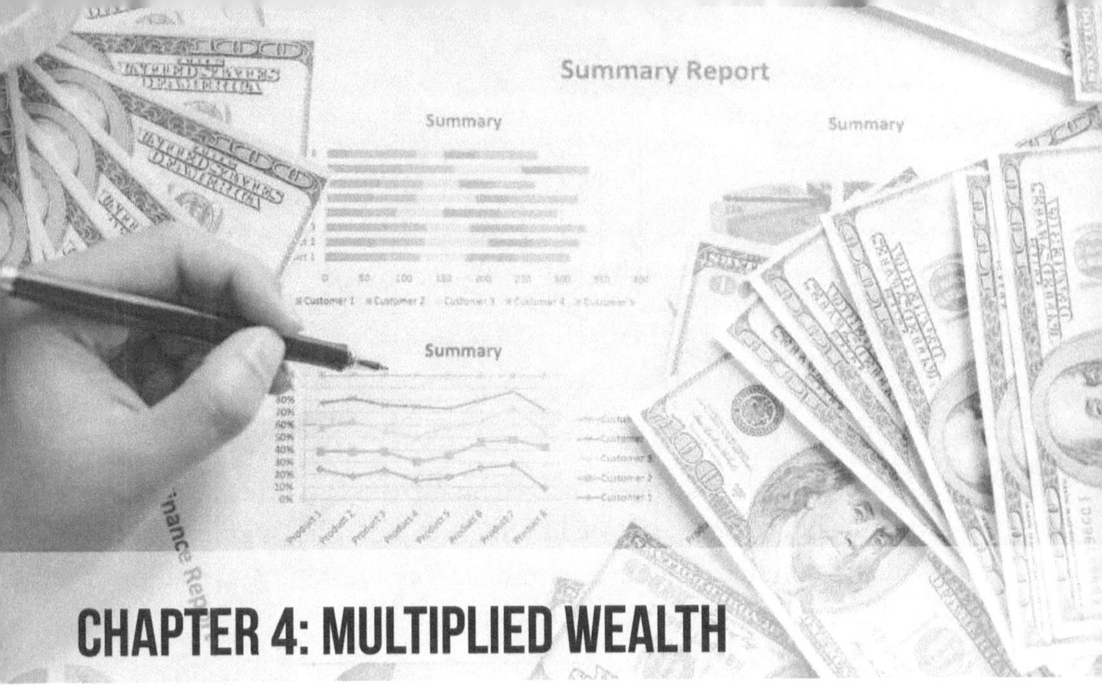

# CHAPTER 4: MULTIPLIED WEALTH

## CREATING AND MANAGING MULTIPLE STREAMS OF INCOME

"The more you learn, the more you earn."
—**Warren Buffett**

S tan felt a sense of pride and accomplishment as he reviewed his various income streams. For years, he had worked tirelessly to build his family practice office, and now, he was finally reaping the rewards.

As a former Army Green Beret, Stan knew the importance of being prepared for any situation. He applied this mentality to his financial strategy, building multiple income streams to protect himself from unexpected events.

His second stream of income was from his real estate investments. Stan was keen to spot lucrative properties and built a solid rental property portfolio. His third income stream was from his physician consulting business, where he provided expert advice to companies looking to improve their operations.

But Stan didn't stop there. He had recently started investing in the stock market, using his extensive knowledge in the medical field and experience to make investments in biotechnology.

Despite his success, Stan remained humble and grounded. He knew that the key to financial freedom was not just about making money but also about managing it wisely. He was constantly learning and seeking advice from experts in different fields.

As he sipped his coffee, Stan reflected on the journey that had led him to this point. It had not been easy, but it had been worth it. His Green Beret military training taught him not to give up and work hard, to take calculated risks, and never give up on his dream of achieving financial freedom.

Tom Clancy once wrote, "The difference between fiction and reality? Fiction has to make sense." For Stan, the reality of building multiple income streams made perfect sense. It was a strategy that brought him financial freedom and the ability to live on his terms.

There are several streams of income that the average person can invest into profit:

- Dividend stocks: Investing in stocks that pay dividends can provide a steady income stream. Dividend stocks are shares in companies that pay a portion of their profits back to shareholders as dividends.

- Rental properties: Owning and renting out property can provide a reliable income stream. This can be an excellent long-term investment, as rental income can increase over time.

- Peer-to-peer lending: This involves lending money to individuals or businesses through online platforms. The borrower pays interest on the loan, providing a source of passive income for the lender.

- High-yield savings accounts: While they don't offer a high return, they are a safe way to invest and earn interest on your money.

- Index funds: These are mutual funds that track a specific market index. They are a low-cost way to invest in a diversified portfolio of stocks and can provide a steady income stream through dividends.

- Side hustles: Starting a side business or freelancing can provide an additional income stream. This can include selling products online, offering a service, or creating content.

Remember that investing always has some risk, and before making any investment decisions, do your research and speak with a financial professional.

# CHAPTER 5: WHY SETTLE FOR ONE?

## THE IMPORTANCE OF MULTIPLE STREAMS OF INCOME

"The richest people in the world look for and build networks; everyone else looks for work."
—**Robert Kiyosaki**

Every person should strive to have at least three or four income streams. This number could increase while in retirement. While teaching thousands of adults, I discovered that most people rely on just one income stream—their job. However, everyone wishes to move toward financial freedom. They want to improve their financial situations and have at least one of two goals:

1. To become a better investor or

2. To earn more income.

As a professor, I am committed to helping people achieve both objectives. This book will focus on specific ways to increase the income flowing into your life.

We are often told that diversification is an essential financial strategy. But we are rarely told about the importance of applying this powerful economic principle to our sources of income. That is what makes this book unique. My goal is to educate, equip, and empower you to develop a diversified portfolio of income streams that will protect you and your family's financial future.

This book will introduce you to the most popular and proven income streams that nearly anyone can follow. I want to share why I am passionate about helping people create multiple income streams. Let's begin by examining how the evolving concept of retirement has dramatically increased the need for multiple income streams for us into our golden years.

## Some Retirement for All

From the dawn of humanity to modern times, every person has grappled with the unpredictability of life, from losing a job to grappling with sickness, disability, and eventually aging. These harsh realities constantly threaten our economic stability, but thankfully, a glimmer of hope emerged in the form of the Social Security Act.

On August 14, 1935, the Social Security Act was passed, creating a new federally run social insurance program for the elderly. This program is funded by payroll taxes paid by both employees and their employers. The government implemented a revolutionary system of social insurance for the elderly. This innovative program was funded by the sweat and toil of employees and their employers, who dutifully paid their fair share of payroll taxes.

The passage of this landmark legislation marked a turning point in history, providing a beacon of hope and financial support for those who had borne the brunt of life's hardships. It was a remarkable achievement, a testament to the resilience and spirit of the American people in the face of adversity. And to this day, Social Security remains a vital lifeline for millions, a shining example of what we can accomplish when we work together for the greater good.

Back in ancient times, the idea of retirement was completely foreign. No record exists of any ancient citizen putting in decades of work only to spend their golden years gallivanting across the countryside in a luxurious horse-drawn "airstream." However, this doesn't mean that people in the past didn't plan for their old age.

Early Greek and Roman investors could buy a "annual," a type of annuity, to secure their income. They could secure a retirement income by buying this financial instrument. It was a smart move that showed ancient people were planning for the future.

Ancient people didn't worry about longevity, and we do today. Instead, our ancient elders had an asset class that could support them after retirement.

What made it special? Children. Children were assets in ancient times. Many elderly Americans "scrimp and save" to leave their families, whom they may not have seen in years, an inheritance. However, children used to care for their elderly parents. Parents with many children were blessed. Kids are never a liability. I joke. Children were once a parent's "retirement plan."

Our "sophisticated" retirement planning expects parents to pay for their children's education and leave them an inheritance! This unsustainable system of parents supporting their children past 18 is failing. As nearly 10,000 Americans retire daily for the next two decades, we are all experiencing a seismic shift.

## I Can't Retire; I'm Too Scared

An analysis of the common methods for funding the cost of retirement in America shows that retirement, as we know, is in grave financial danger. Social Security is in a crisis. Based on current projections, we already know that without massive intervention, the Social Security program will be insolvent before 2033.

The Medicare program, which millions of retired Americans rely on for healthcare, is facing a funding shortfall. This is happening as the baby boomer generation is retiring at a rate of over 10,000 individuals per day. Due to a combination of rising medical costs and financial mismanagement, the healthcare system is projected to become insolvent earlier than expected.

Our pensions system is also underfunded and failing. Under the weight of poor market performance, years of low yields, and unsound financial management, many large government and corporate pension plans are woefully underfunded. A report released by the pension consulting firm Milliman shows that public US companies' 100 most significant pension funds had a record funding shortfall of over 300 billion dollars. To make matters worse, the Pension Benefit Guaranty Corporation (PBGC)—the government agency that covers retiree benefits when companies go bankrupt, and their pensions fail—is bankrupt (Klein, E.,2020). For millions of American workers, this spells disaster. What seemed "a good idea then "has become unsustainable.

Our saving rate is bleakly low. In early 2012, the US personal savings rate stood at 3.7%. Over 25% of American workers admit to having no personal savings whatsoever. The Consumption Trap seems to have effectively indoctrinated Americans to spend all they earn.

According to Morrissey (2019), the Bureau of Labor Statistics reports that only 67% of workers have access to employer-sponsored retirement accounts, such as 401k, 403BS, and individual retirement savings plans, which are underutilized. Today, according to the bureau of labor statistics, only 67% of workers have access to employer-sponsored retirement accounts. And due to a severe lack of personal savings, many Americans with a retirement plan have used it as a piggy bank during difficult financial times. And as of this writing, less than four in ten Americans have an Individual Retirement Account (IRA).

Consumer credit card and debt levels are interfering with our retirement savings. Increasing consumer debt has caused many Americans to decrease their retirement savings to service their debt obligations. In addition, reports of Americans carrying massive debt loads into retirement are sadly becoming more common. As of the writing of this book, the inflation rate is at 6.5%, and it also increases the amount of credit card debt, which is tied to inflation.

As I write this book, continued advances in medical technology have increased the risk of outliving our money. Who could have imagined that long life would be viewed as a curse? However, numerous studies show that the greatest fear most Baby Boomers share is not death but outliving their savings and money. Unfortunately, this is a real fear given our nation's low savings rates and overconsumption, coupled with ongoing medical advancements increasing the average lifespan. I would like to reach 100, so I can brag about it, but I would rather pass away peacefully if my mental state is not in tack. Put simply, most people are broke. We have too much debt and are

NOT saving enough; what we have saved is at risk.

## The Importance of Creating Multiple Streams of Income

Never depend on a single income. Make investments to create a second source." —***Warren Buffett***

Over time, investing in the stock market has long been considered one of the most powerful ways to build wealth. But with so many different investment options available, it can be overwhelming to know where to start. One of the most important things you can do is learn about the various income streams for investing to make informed decisions and maximize your returns.

One of the best streams of income for investing is dividend investing. Dividends are payments made by companies to their shareholders and can provide a reliable source of passive income. By investing in stocks that pay high dividends, you can create a steady stream of income that can help you achieve your financial goals.

Another great stream of income is investing in real estate. Real estate can provide a steady income stream through rental properties or Real Estate Investment Trusts (REITs). Rental properties can generate rental income and appreciate over time, while REITs offer exposure to a diversified portfolio of real estate assets and provide regular dividend payments to investors.

In addition to dividend investing and real estate, there are many other streams of income to explore, such as bonds, annuities, and options trading. Bonds are fixed-income investments that can provide regular interest payments and a predictable income stream.

Annuities are another type of fixed-income investment that can provide guaranteed income for a fixed period or a lifetime. Options trading is a more advanced strategy that involves buying and selling options contracts to generate revenue from market movements.

Achieving financial freedom is a goal that many of us aspire to, but the path to getting it is not always clear. It's a challenging but straightforward journey that anyone can follow with the right mindset, knowledge, and a relentless drive to succeed. For over a decade, I've been passionate about sharing my expertise with university students and people from all walks of life, helping them understand the critical role of wise financial investing in achieving their financial goals.

It's no secret that building wealth requires discipline, perseverance, and a solid understanding of financial principles. But with the right mindset and knowledge, anyone can start investing in their future and take meaningful steps toward financial freedom. Whether you're just starting or well on your way, the principles of wise financial investing apply to everyone.

My mission is to empower individuals with the knowledge and tools to make intelligent financial decisions that will have a lasting impact on their lives. From budgeting and saving to investing in the stock market, I've seen firsthand the transformative power of sound financial planning. And I'm committed to helping others achieve the same level of success.

So, if you're ready to take control of your financial future, start by learning about the principles of wise financial investing. With a positive attitude and a burning passion for success, you can build the foundation for a lifetime of financial freedom and independence.

Learning about the best income streams for investing is essential for building a successful investment strategy. Understanding the risks involved and diversifying your portfolio by investing in various income-producing assets is important. By educating yourself and seeking expert advice, you can create a balanced and resilient investment strategy that generates income and grows over time. With dedication and a commitment to learning, you can achieve your financial goals and build a secure financial future.

It is no secret that reaching financial freedom is not easy. However, it is a very straightforward process that anyone can apply if they have the right knowledge, a positive attitude, and a burning passion for success. Since I started teaching University students over a decade ago, I have been on a mission to help people from all walks of life understand the importance of wise financial investing.

At the core of my financial teaching lay four basic principles.

1.  Saving regularly each month,

2.  Getting and staying out of bad debt (some debt is good),

3.  Having multiple streams of income or passive income, and

4.  Employing diversification.

In today's fast pace and problematic economy, developing multiple income streams from different sources is more important than ever. Never in our nation's history have so many Americans been one paycheck away from bankruptcy or foreclosure on their homes. What about you? If you lost your primary employment, would you still have an income flowing into your life one month from now? How about six months from now? Who would sign your paycheck if you were in an accident and laid on the couch for an extended period? If you cannot answer these questions, you are not alone. You are in the majority. I hope that through the knowledge presented in this book, you will be able to shift yourself and your family into the minority of those who rely not on one or two income sources but upon multiple streams of income.

You will want to build passive income, this refers to any income that is earned without requiring active involvement or ongoing effort from the investor. In the context of investing, passive income typically refers to investments that generate regular income with little ongoing effort on the part of the investor.

One example of passive income in investing is rental income from real estate properties. If an investor purchases a property and rents it out, they can generate passive income in the form of monthly rental payments. Similarly, investing in dividend-paying stocks or bonds can also generate passive income in the form of regular dividends or interest payments.

Passive income can be an attractive investment strategy because it can provide a steady stream of income without requiring ongoing effort or active management on the part of the investor.

It is time to begin diversifying your income by adding another income stream. Just as spreading your investments across various asset classes is wise, it is also wise to diversify your income. As the old saying goes, "Don't put all of your eggs in one basket." By diversifying your income by creating multiple income streams, you will place a safety net under you and your family in the event of unforeseen circumstances. People with diversified income sources don't feel trapped in jobs they hate and are no longer at the mercy of their employers. When you create multiple income streams, the financial stresses of life will become easier to manage because you will know that if one income stream suddenly dries up, other steady sources continue to flow into your bank account! Today, the average American working household has three income streams. Typically, this includes two W-2 incomes (husband and wife) and interest from a savings account, money market account, or a bank CD.

I do not want to imagine the financial stress of only two or three income streams, especially in this challenging economic climate. And besides, why should any household have just two or three income streams when financial advisors tell us that it is possible to have multiple income streams in retirement? In my research, virtually anyone can create many potential income streams.

I don't understand why someone would work hard for their entire life only to end up with just one- or two income streams when so many more are available for those who will just put forth a little effort. I am often asked, "How many income streams should a person have?" I believe every individual should have a minimum of three income streams (including their regular job) during their working years. In retirement, that number should be increased to a minimum of five income streams. Of course, even more, if you can create, that is preferred. Another question I often get is, "Don't you have to have a lot of money to create multiple income streams?" The short answer is no. You do not need a lot of money to create multiple income streams. But if you lack money, you must replace it with time, a positive attitude, and a willingness to work hard. Over the years, I have created several passive income streams, which flow into our bank account monthly, regardless of whether we work. Remember that my other income streams do not require me to live in any city or area. I am free to travel almost as I wish. But these income streams were not easy to create and did not just magically appear in our lives (Too many people today want to make money without working for it. If that describes you, I am sorry to admit that I cannot help you). For my wife and I to create these income streams, we had to develop a long-term mindset. Why? Because there have been times when I have worked for several weeks or months, and in a few cases even years, for little or no money to properly develop an income stream. However, once I finally built the income stream, it began cash-flowing regularly with just a little maintenance.

## Focus on Trends and your Strengths When Developing Income Streams

Over the last 60 years, the technology industry has undergone an incredible transformation, changing how we live, work, and communicate. From the early days of mainframe computers to the present-day smartphone revolution, technology has made our lives more convenient, efficient, and enjoyable.

One of the most significant trends in the technology industry has been the rise of the internet and the proliferation of mobile devices. This has allowed people to connect in previously unimaginable ways. It has also created an explosion in digital content, giving rise to new business models and income streams.

Approximately 90.1% of Americans had internet connectivity as of 2021, according to data from the World Bank. But, depending on variables like age, income, education, and geography, this percentage may change.

It's vital to keep in mind that not every place in the United States has access to the Internet equally; some areas can have lower prices than others. The COVID-19 epidemic has also brought attention to the differences in internet access and digital literacy that already exist, with some groups being disproportionately impacted.

Generally, the proportion of Americans who have access to the Internet is higher than in many other nations, but more needs to be done to guarantee that everyone can use this vital instrument for economic opportunity, education, and communication.

As the technology industry has grown and evolved, so too have the opportunities for individuals to develop their own income streams. Whether through app development, content creation, or e-commerce, there are countless ways to turn a passion for technology into a profitable business.

One strength of the technology industry is its ability to innovate and adapt to changing circumstances constantly. This means there are always new opportunities for entrepreneurs to develop income streams. For example, the emergence of blockchain technology has created a whole new ecosystem of startups and businesses; all focused on building the infrastructure for a decentralized future.

Another strength of the technology industry is its global reach. With the internet, it is now possible to reach customers and clients from all over the world. This creates an enormous potential market for anyone looking to develop an income stream in technology.

Overall, the last 60 years of technological innovation have created an incredible opportunity for individuals to develop income streams in the industry. With a focus on innovation, adaptation, and global reach, there is no telling what the future of technology will hold and what new opportunities it will create for those looking to develop their income streams.

Technology that changed us: 60 Years of Breakthroughs

- 1950: Mainframe computers 1952, IBM's first large computer based on the vacuum tube

- 1960: transforming science fiction into fact. Robots, satellites, and the moon landing

- In the 1970s, from Pong to Apollo, ATMs and Credit cards

- In the 1980s, from MS-DOS to the first GPS satellite

- In the 1990s, from WorldWideWeb / Internet to Google

- In the 2000s, from iPhone to Twitter

- In the 2010s, Fintech Revolution, Bitcoin, and Crypto

On your path toward financial freedom, you will unavoidably undergo a trial and error-process. But this is a vital filtering process that will help you discover your true strengths and weaknesses. It took me years to discover my strengths. My weaknesses, on the other hand, were easy to determine! I remember middle and high school kids who had their whole life planned out. That was not me. And this "cluelessness" about my future did not just plague my Childhood … I virtually stumbled through my college years without knowing exactly where I was going. Fortunately, my work ethic was a strength that others would recognize. My leadership abilities helped me quickly move into management positions and progress in my career in Information Technology.

Then in the midst of the 2008 recession which was the worst economic downturn in modern history, life dealt me a tough blow. The company I had dedicated myself to for years merged with a larger out-of-state company, leading to mass layoffs and leaving me without a job.

After losing my job I worked tirelessly to build my own business. I enjoyed the process of starting and expanding a new business venture. I was incredibly enthused about coming up with ideas, launching, and building a new business and source of revenue. The company did not, however, grow to the point where it could generate the kind of cash I required to support my six children. And while it was a challenging time, I never lost hope. I turned to teaching part-time to make ends meet. However, I was not alone in my journey. My loving wife,  stood by my side every step of the way, bringing in much-needed income as a nurse. Together, we were a team, and we were determined to find a way to secure our financial future.

That's when we first turned to real estate. We saw the potential to generate passive income through rental properties, and we didn't hesitate to jump in. It wasn't easy - there were hurdles to overcome and risks to take - but with our shared vision and unwavering commitment, we made it work.

Through it all, we learned that investing is truly a team sport, especially when you're married.  We relied on each other's strengths and supported each other through tough times, and we emerged stronger than ever before.

Our story is a testament to the power of resilience and teamwork, and it's one that we hope would inspire others to never give up, no matter how tough the odds may seem.

## The Technology and Innovations Coming Together this Decade

The world constantly evolves, and technology plays a significant role in shaping our lives. As we move into a new decade, imagining the future is fascinating. Several emerging technologies are poised to disrupt how we do things, and I believe they will define this decade. In this book, I  discuss five of these future disruptive technologies and their potential impact on society.

## Public Blockchain, Smart Contracts, and Cryptocurrencies

Public blockchain technology is a way to make transactions that are both safe and open. It works like a decentralized ledger. Smart contracts are agreements that are written into computer code and then automatically carry out their terms. Cryptocurrencies are digital currencies that use encryption to control the creation of new units of currency and verify the transfer of funds. These technologies could change the way we do business, especially in industries like banking and real estate that rely heavily on middlemen. By eliminating the need for middlemen, blockchain technology can cut costs, improve efficiency, and make things clearer. Using smart contracts can also automate complicated tasks, which lowers the risk of fraud and mistakes. Cryptocurrencies are an alternative to traditional currencies, and because they are decentralized, they can be used by more people.

## Artificial Intelligence

Artificial intelligence refers to the development of computer systems that can do tasks that ordinarily require human intelligence, such as speech recognition, decision-making, and language translation (AI).

AI can potentially revolutionize various industries, from healthcare to manufacturing to transportation. In healthcare, AI can help diagnose diseases and develop personalized treatment plans. In manufacturing, AI can optimize production processes and reduce waste. In transportation, AI can improve traffic flow and reduce accidents. The possibilities are endless, and as AI technology evolves, its potential applications will only continue to grow.

A recent example of AI is ChatGPT which launched in Nov 2022. Based on the GPT-3 architecture, OpenAI made ChatGPT a big language model. It uses algorithms for deep learning to respond like a person to a wide range of questions and prompts. Simply put, it can talk to people in a way similar to how people talk to each other.

ChatGPT has already made a big impact in many ways. It has changed how machines can understand human language and respond in a way that sounds natural and makes sense. This has opened up new opportunities in areas like customer service, chatbots, and virtual assistants, where ChatGPT can answer questions immediately and improve the user experience.

ChatGPT has also been used in different research fields to find new ideas and insights. It has been used, for example, to make new drug compounds, improve language translation, and even make new works of art. This could change how we conduct research and development in many fields, making it faster and more effective.

Overall, ChatGPT has had a big impact. It has opened up new ways for people to interact with machines and changed how we think about language processing and research.

## Multiplex Sequencing of DNA

Multiplex sequencing of DNA refers to the ability to sequence multiple genes simultaneously. This technology allows for the rapid and accurate analysis of genetic information, which has the potential to revolutionize the field of medicine.

By analyzing a patient's genetic makeup, doctors can develop personalized treatment plans tailored to their specific needs. This can lead to better outcomes, fewer side effects, and reduced healthcare costs. Additionally, multiplex sequencing can help identify genetic predispositions to diseases, allowing for early intervention and prevention.

## Energy Storage

Energy storage refers to the ability to store energy for later use. This technology is crucial for developing renewable energy sources, such as solar and wind power, which are inherently intermittent.

As energy storage technology improves, relying on renewable energy sources for our energy needs will become increasingly feasible. This will reduce our dependence on fossil fuels, reduce greenhouse gas emissions, and help combat climate change.

## Robotics

Robotics refers to developing robots that can perform tasks autonomously or with minimal human input. Robotic technology is rapidly advancing, becoming increasingly sophisticated and capable.

Robotics can potentially revolutionize various industries, from manufacturing to healthcare to transportation. Robots can perform repetitive tasks faster and more accurately than humans in manufacturing. In healthcare, robots can assist with surgeries and provide care to patients. In transportation, robots can drive vehicles autonomously, reducing the risk of accidents and improving efficiency.

The disruptive technologies of the future have the potential to revolutionize our society in numerous ways. These technologies are the future investment catalyst. The public blockchain, smart contracts, and cryptocurrencies have the potential to transform the way we conduct transactions. Artificial intelligence can revolutionize various industries, from healthcare to manufacturing to transportation. Multiplex sequencing of DNA can help develop personalized treatment plans and identify genetic predispositions to diseases. Energy storage can help us transition to renewable energy sources and combat

## Your Personal SWOT Analysis

Conducting a SWOT analysis on oneself can be an incredibly powerful tool for personal development and growth. SWOT stands for Strengths, Weaknesses, Opportunities, and Threats. The process involves taking a comprehensive look at one's personal and professional characteristics to identify areas for improvement and potential avenues for success.

One of the significant benefits of conducting a SWOT analysis on oneself is that it provides an opportunity to reflect on personal strengths and weaknesses. By identifying strengths, one can gain greater self-awareness and build on those strengths to enhance personal and professional performance. Conversely, identifying weaknesses allows one to focus on areas that need improvement and take steps to address them.

In addition to looking at personal characteristics, a SWOT analysis can identify opportunities and threats in one's environment. This can help individuals to be more aware of their surroundings and make more informed decisions about their personal and professional lives. Identifying opportunities can lead to new avenues for success while identifying threats can help anticipate and mitigate potential obstacles.

Conducting a SWOT analysis on oneself is not only valuable for personal growth but also for career development and investing. Knowing one's strengths and weaknesses can inform decisions about career paths, job opportunities, and investing, while identifying opportunities and threats in the job market can inform one's career strategy.

The power of conducting a SWOT analysis on oneself lies in its opportunity for self-reflection, self-awareness, and informed decision-making. By identifying personal strengths and weaknesses, opportunities and threats in one's environment, individuals can gain greater control over their lives and make more informed decisions about their personal and professional goals. The primary purpose of SWOT analysis is to increase awareness of the factors that go into making up our inventory. Here are just some of the examples of a SWOT analysis:

Strengths

- List advantages you have over others (for example, skills, certifications, education, or connections).

- What do you excel at or perform best at?

- What private resources are available to you?

- What other accomplishments are you the most proud of?

Weaknesses:

- What chores do you typically avoid because you lack confidence in completing them?

- What flaws will those around you perceive in you?

- Do you have complete faith in the education and training you've received? Where are you most vulnerable if not?

- What are your bad work habits (such as being frequently late, being disorganized, having a bad temper, or having trouble managing stress)?

- Do you possess personality traits that limit you in your profession? For instance, if you frequently conduct meetings, your fear of public speaking might be significant.

Opportunities:

- What cutting-edge technologies can you use? Or can you use the Internet to contact people or others for assistance?

- Is your industry growing? If so, how can you take advantage of the current market?

- Is your sector expanding? If that's the case, how can you profit from the current market?

- Do you have a network of influential people who can support you or provide wise counsel?

Threats:

- What challenges are you currently dealing with in your life?

- How many hours a week do you work?

- Is your position threatened by evolving technology?

- Could any of your weaknesses lead to threats?

- Could any of your flaws expose you to danger?

If we make the most of our talents, we can be successful. According to this, we will experience fewer issues if we are aware of our shortcomings and control them so they don't affect our work. You should identify your strengths and weaknesses, as knowing how to move forward on the road to financial freedom is vital.

Because I was a "late bloomer," it took a while for me to discover my gifts and talents. Let that encourage those who feel you are too old or not smart enough to start something new. Don't use your educational level, ethnicity, age, or any other factor, as an excuse. Keep in mind that most all things are possible for those who believe. You have skills, gifts, talents, and life experiences. You are unique and were placed on this earth for a reason. You have a special purpose. You just must put one foot in front of the other. Don't expect anyone to do it for you. Breaking free financially will take time and effort, but it will be worth every second of your time. You will not always succeed at every new idea or concept. But don't let that stand in your way of achieving financial success. Pace yourself and move boldly in the direction of your goals and dreams. For example, with every new income stream I build, I set reasonable goals that I know can be achieved. I would celebrate with some of my first income streams when they began creating $100.00 monthly! Then a few months later, when the income stream would start creating more money per month, I would celebrate again. If you walk into this endeavor with unrealistic expectations of making millions of dollars within a few months, your chances of failure will increase dramatically. So be humble and work hard. Set reasonable goals. If you spend time developing and working on systems that work, you will succeed with time. If I can do it, you can too!

We can break income types into active (paycheck), portfolio, and passive.

## Active Income

Income earned while providing a service is referred to as active income. Active income includes things like wages, tips, salaries, commissions, and money from businesses where you have a material stake. In other words, active income is the remuneration you receive on a biweekly basis for your work, employment, or material investment in a firm. Moreover, it could consist of wages (W-2 income), sales commissions, tips, consulting revenue, and more. The type of income with the highest tax rate is active income.

## Portfolio Income

Dividends, interest, royalties, and capital gains are all sources of portfolio income. For example, you might acquire stock in a company cheaply and then sell it for a profit when its value rises. This is a capital gain that falls under the heading of portfolio income. Portfolio income could also come from royalties earned from books or patents. The important thing to remember is that this kind of money is not produced through routine business operations. As a result, depending on how long you hold an investment before selling it, portfolio income is frequently taxed at a lower rate than active income.

## Passive Income

Passive income is a financial concept that has recently gained immense popularity. It refers to the money earned without active involvement in any trade or profession. This may sound too good to be true, but the reality is that passive income is not only possible but also a viable source of financial stability and freedom.

One of the most significant advantages of passive income is that it allows people to earn money while pursuing other passions or goals. Whether writing a book, traveling the world, or starting a new business, passive income can provide a steady stream of cash flow without the need for constant active participation.

Moreover, passive income sources require minimal effort to set up and maintain, making them an excellent choice for those seeking financial independence without sacrificing their time and energy. Examples of passive income streams include rental income, stock dividends, interest from savings accounts, and royalties from creative works.

Investing in passive income can also help people build long-term wealth, as they allow for consistent earnings and the potential for compound interest over time. With a diverse portfolio of passive income streams, individuals can enjoy the benefits of financial stability and security for years to come.

In addition to being a sustainable and dependable source of income, passive income offers a road to financial freedom and the freedom to pursue one's interests and passions without jeopardizing one's financial security. Individuals can build a life of financial freedom, security, and wealth by investing in passive income streams.

Passive income is regular earnings from a source other than an employer or contractor. The Internal Revenue Service (IRS) explains that passive income can come from either rental property or a business that a person is not actively involved in, like earning stock dividends or book royalties. Passive income is produced by investments in companies you are not actively involved with, like limited partnerships or rental properties. According to the IRS, only two types of passive income are permitted: net rental income (from property or equipment) and commercial income from a business in which you have no significant ownership stake. Passive money cannot be "earned" using your time and effort. The greatest possible tax deductions are available from passive income, which is frequently taxed at the lowest rates.

## Your 401k

Investing in your company's 401k plan is one of the most powerful financial decisions you can make for your future. A 401k plan is a tax-advantaged retirement savings plan that allows you to contribute a portion of your salary to an account that will grow tax-free until you retire. While many people are hesitant to invest in their 401k plan, there are many reasons why it is an innovative and compelling choice.

First and foremost, investing in your company's 401k plan allows you to take control of your retirement savings. With Social Security benefits becoming increasingly uncertain, retirement savings is more important than ever. By contributing to your 401k plan, you are taking responsibility for your financial future and setting yourself up for a comfortable retirement.

Another compelling reason to invest in your 401k plan is its tax benefits. When you contribute to your 401k, you do not pay taxes on that money until you withdraw it in retirement. This means your money can grow tax-free for many years, compounding over time and potentially earning significant returns. Additionally, many employers offer a matching contribution to your 401k, essentially free money you should take advantage of.

The amount of money companies match for your 401k plan varies depending on the employer and the plan's specific terms. Typically, companies will match a certain percentage of your contributions up to a certain limit.

For example, an employer may offer to match 50% of your contributions up to a maximum of 6% of your salary. This means that if you contribute 6% of your 401k plan, your employer will contribute 3% of your salary.

Some employers may also offer a dollar-for-dollar match up to a certain percentage of your salary. Reviewing your company's specific 401k plan documents or speaking with your HR representative to understand the details of your plan's matching contribution is important.

It's important to note that while employer matching contributions are a great benefit, they should not be the only factor to consider when deciding how much to contribute to your 401k plan. You should aim to contribute as much as possible to save for retirement, even if your employer does not offer a matching contribution.

While Roth 401(k) IRS deductions differ. Roth 401(k) and Roth IRA contributions use taxed money (IRA). Retirement withdrawals and profits grow tax-free. If you remove money before 59.5, a typical 401(k) involves taxes and a 10% penalty. Roth 401(k) non-qualified withdrawals match contributions and profits. Gross income funds have a 10% early withdrawal penalty.

Roth and conventional 401(k)s must start RMDs at 72. (if you hit 7012 in 2019 or earlier). Changing your Roth 401(k) to a Roth IRA without RMDs before retirement eliminates this need. Hence, your IRA can grow tax-free, and your heirs won't pay taxes on withdrawals.

"This flexibility is a huge distinction between Roth and standard 401(k)s or IRAs," says Schwab Center for Financial Research managing director of financial planning, retirement income, and asset management Rob Williams (Williams, R).

401(k)s may not be essential (k). Roth and regular 401(k) contributions are allowed if your company allows them (k). Roth contributions are tax-deferred, while ordinary contributions go directly into your account. Your employer can match both.

Both accounts have an annual contribution restriction. Each 401(k) cannot exceed the 2022 salary deferral limit of $20,500 (or $27,000 if you are 50 or older) (k). Instead, deposit $10,000 and $10,500. Your yearly contribution with employer matching ($61,000 or $67,500 if 50 or older) is the same.

## Saving

Investing in your 401k plan also allows you to diversify your investments. Many plans offer a range of investment options, such as mutual funds or target-date funds, enabling you to spread your investments across different asset classes and reduce your risk. This is important because investing in just one asset, such as a single stock, can be risky and can result in significant losses.

Finally, investing in your 401k plan is easy and convenient. Your contributions are automatically deducted from your paycheck, so you don't have to worry about remembering to make deposits or investments on your own. This can help you stay on track with your savings goals and consistently save for retirement.

Investing in your company's 401k plan is a compelling financial decision that can set you up for a comfortable and secure retirement. With tax benefits, diversification, and convenience, many reasons exist to take advantage of this important investment opportunity. By contributing to your 401k plan, you are taking control of your financial future and setting yourself up for success. Don't wait. Start investing in your 401k plan today.

## The importance of diversification

By distributing assets among different financial instruments, industries, and other categories, diversification is an approach to lowering risk. It tries to optimize return by investing in various sectors that ought to respond to changes in market conditions differently. Diversification is often explained as "not putting all your eggs in one basket." Many well-known investors, including Warren Buffett, have repeated this opinion. According to Cardinal Retirement Planning's chief investment officer, Anessa Custovic, "Diversification in investing implies you have more baskets. You won't crack all the eggs if there are several baskets of them.

According to academic definitions, diversification is the process of choosing and arranging a portfolio's investment assets to minimize exposure to risk sources. "Every financial instrument is subject to certain risk factors, and a portfolio that is overly concentrated in a single instrument (or group of instruments with similar risk profiles) tends to be much more sensitive to those risk factors and more volatile as a result," says Julia Spina, quantitative finance researcher at TastyTrade. "The more volatile the returns of a portfolio, the harder it is for investors to develop reliable profit expectations."

Some of the risks to be aware of include the following:

1.  Market risk: How the overall stock market movements affect your returns. This is also known as systemic risk and is unavoidable if you invest in assets other than cash.

2.  Interest rate risk: How changes in interest rates affect your returns and yields, especially for fixed-income assets (for example, how long-term Treasuries suffer when rates rise).

3.  Geographical risk: How changes in political or social regimes affect a particular market's equities and fixed-income assets (for example, in the recent Russian stock market collapse).

4.  Idiosyncratic risk: How specific changes in the fundamentals of any one company can affect its stock returns (for example, if you were invested in Enron before it declared bankruptcy).

Your portfolio will often be more diversified and resistant to various risk kinds as it contains more assets. According to Jennifer Sireklove, managing director of investment strategy at Parametric Portfolio Associates, "Diversification is aiming to own every imaginable sort of investment in the market in the most extreme version." (Sireklove, J.)

## Benefits of diversification

Two academic ideas, correlation and variance/standard deviation, lie at the core of diversification. The amount and direction of the relationship between the returns on two assets are measured by correlation. When two assets have a correlation of 1, they move precisely in the same direction, and when they move perfectly in opposite directions, the correlation is 1. When there is no linkage between two assets, they move independently of one another. Standard deviation and variance measure the historical range of an asset that fluctuates, on average, around its expected return. For example, suppose a stock has returned a compound average growth rate, or CAGR, of 7% annually. In that case, it has a high variance (and, therefore, a high standard deviation, the square root of variance). This means its return varies widely, and 7% might not be a reasonable expectation in any given year.

A rule of thumb is that a diversified portfolio of volatile (high standard deviation) and uncorrelated (between 0.20 and 0.50) assets with positive expected returns will produce a better risk-return profile than an undiversified portfolio of a single asset.

## The dollar-cost averaging strategy

Dollar-cost averaging regularly invests a fixed dollar amount, regardless of the share price. It's an excellent way to develop a disciplined investing habit, be more efficient, and potentially lower your stress level and overall share costs. Dollar-Cost Averaging is a strategy to manage price risk when purchasing equities, exchange-traded funds (ETFs), or mutual funds. By dividing the amount of money you want to spend into smaller, more frequent purchases over time, dollar cost averaging allows you to invest in a given investment over time rather than all at once at a single purchase price. By using this tactic, the risk of paying too much before market prices fall is reduced.

Of course, prices don't always go in one direction the price can move up or down. Also, dollar cost averaging enables you to continuously put your money to work, which is essential for long-term investment success. Using dollar cost averaging every two weeks is probably already a habit if you have a corporate retirement plan, such as a 401(k).

To sum up the advantages of DCA, employing DCA enables you to expand your portfolio without attempting to time the market or purchase the drop. Instead, you can use an automatic trading platform to set up repeated purchases.

## DCA Summary

- Reduces the impact of volatility in the market, securing you an average price
- Less emotion clouding your buying decisions
- It saves you time from manually setting up buy orders
- It allows you to manage your budget instead of investing a lump sum gradually

## Market Timing vs. Dollar Cost Averaging

One of the most effective and simple investment methods, dollar-cost averaging is perfect for individual investors. Because asset prices often increase over the long term, it is effective. The S&P 500 has increased in value in 40 out of the last 50 years, producing an average annualized return of 9.4%, according to Fool.com. Asset prices do not, however, rise steadily in the foreseeable future. Instead, they chase after transient highs and lows that might not conform to any pattern. It eliminates a great deal of guesswork and simplifies investing. It is unlikely to work out even if you could theoretically earn bigger returns if you are a skilled stock market timer. Dollar-cost averaging can help investors detach themselves from their emotions.

Several people have tried to time the market and purchase assets at low prices. In principle, this seems simple enough. Even for experienced stock pickers, predicting how the market will behave in the near future is practically difficult. The price that is low today can be high the next week. Moreover, a month from now, this week's high may appear to be a low.

Every item can only be priced favorably in the rearview mirror; at that time, it is too late to buy. When you try to time your asset acquisition by waiting on the sidelines, you usually buy at a price that has plateaued after the asset has already experienced significant gains.

Yet trying to time the market can be expensive. According to research by Charles Schwab, investors who tried to time the market had much smaller gains than those who consistently invested via dollar cost averaging (Charles Schwab).

## How Does Dollar Cost Averaging Work?

By continually spending the same little amount on an item, dollar-cost averaging removes the emotional component of investing. This implies that you purchase more shares at low prices and less shares at high prices.

Let's say you want to put $3,600 into Mutual Fund A this year. You have two options: $300 every month, or investing all of your money at once. Although it might not seem like much of a difference either method you choose, if you stretch out your purchases over 12 months in $300 monthly increments, you might wind up owning more shares than you would if you bought everything at once.

## Should You Use Dollar Cost Averaging?

You should consider dollar cost averaging:

1. If you are new to investing in stocks or cryptocurrencies and only have tiny amounts to purchase shares, you should think about dollar cost averaging.

2. If you have a lack of interest in the extensive studies that support market timing.

3. If you make regular monthly investments in retirement accounts, like an IRA or a 401(k).

4. If you are unlikely to keep investing in down markets.

5. If you want to set up your investments and deal with them infrequently

# SECTION III:
# GET STARTED WITH TRADING STOCKS

# WHERE DO I START

## CHAPTER 6: STOCK MARKET 101

### A BEGINNER'S GUIDE TO TRADING AND INVESTING

> "The stock market is a device for transferring money from the impatient to the patient." —**Warren Buffett**

As a young man, I had always been fascinated by the world of finance. I spent countless hours poring over the financial news, studying the stock market, and dreaming of the day I could be a successful trader. But I lacked the funds and confidence to dive in and start trading for years.

That all changed when I stumbled upon a copy of "How to Make Money in Stocks" by legendary trader William J. O'Neil. As I devoured the book, I felt my confidence grow. O'Neil's clear, concise writing style made even the most complex financial concepts easy to understand. Armed with the knowledge I had gained from the book, I began trading with small amounts of money, carefully managing my risk and constantly analyzing my trades. At first, I made some mistakes and suffered losses, but I refused to give up. Over time, my persistence and hard work paid off. I became increasingly skilled at picking winning stocks, and my profits grew. Before long, I was able to turn a small investment into a much larger one.

But for me, the real reward was not just the money. It was the knowledge that I had overcome my fears and learned to master the stock market. I had achieved something that had once seemed impossible, and I knew that the lessons I had learned would stay with me for the rest of my life.

Looking back on my journey, I could hardly believe how far I had come. But I knew I owed it all to the book that had changed my investing knowledge and the determination and hard work that had built my confidence in stock trading.

## Stock Market Indexes

*Figure 4*

The DOW, S&P, and NASDAQ are all stock market indices that track the performance of a specific group of stocks. Here's a brief explanation of each:

1. The oldest and best-known stock market index is the Dow Jones Industrial Average (DOW). It consists of 30 large publicly traded businesses from several sectors, including Apple, Microsoft, and Coca-Cola. The index is produced by dividing the total stock prices of the 30 companies by a factor that takes stock splits and other changes into account. Investors, analysts, and the media carefully monitor the DOW as a proxy for the state of the U.S. stock market as a whole. In addition, many mutual funds and other investment products use it as a benchmark.

2. Standard & Poor's 500 (S&P 500): The S&P 500 is an index of 500 large-cap American firms that measure the stock market's performance. Market capitalization, liquidity, and other considerations are used to select these businesses. Since the index is weighted according to market size, the performance of the largest companies has the biggest impact on the index. Because it contains a wider variety of firms and is weighted by market capitalization, the S&P 500 is frequently seen as a more realistic representation of the American stock market than the Dow. It serves as a benchmark for many financial products and is closely watched by investors, experts, and the media.

3. NASDAQ Composite Index (NASDAQ): The NASDAQ is an index of the stock market that measures the performance of more than 3,000 businesses that are traded on the NASDAQ stock exchange. Several technological advancements and

growth-oriented businesses like Amazon, Facebook, and Google are represented in the index. The NASDAQ is often considered a barometer of the technology sector's performance and is closely followed by investors, analysts, and the media. It is also a benchmark for many investment products focusing on technology and growth-oriented companies.

Overall, investors and analysts follow these indices because they provide a snapshot of the stock market's overall performance, as well as specific sectors and industries. They can be used as a benchmark for investment performance and help investors make informed decisions about where to allocate their money. This index, which mostly focuses on technology, covers the roughly 3,000 companies that are a part of the NASDAQ stock market. Leading biotech and technology companies like Apple, Google, and Microsoft are among them. Since the index began including 500 stocks in 1957 and up through 2018, the average yearly return has been about 8%.

## Online Brokers

Online brokers are financial institutions that enable investors to trade securities, such as stocks, bonds, and mutual funds, over the internet. They provide a platform for investors to buy and sell securities, access market research, and manage their investments from the comfort of their own homes or offices.

One of the most significant benefits of using online brokers is convenience. Investors no longer need to physically visit a broker's office to trade securities or have a face-to-face conversation with a broker. Instead, they can access their investment accounts anywhere, anytime, using a computer or mobile device. This means investors can quickly react to changes in the market, execute trades instantly, and manage their investments at their own pace.

Online brokers also offer access to a wealth of market research and educational resources. Many online brokers provide tools and resources to help investors make informed decisions, such as real-time market data, company profiles, and financial news. They also offer educational resources, such as webinars and online courses, to help investors improve their investment knowledge and skills.

Another benefit of using online brokers is the lower fees and commissions. Online brokers typically charge lower fees than traditional brokers, making it more affordable for investors to trade securities. This means investors can keep more of their investment returns, which can compound over time to build long-term wealth.

Online brokers are a convenient and cost-effective way for investors to trade securities, manage their investments, and access market research and educational resources. With the ease of use, low fees, and vast resources available, online brokers are an excellent choice for novice and experienced investors looking to build their investment portfolios. Here is a short list of some of the well-known brokers:

1. Fidelity: Fidelity is a brokerage firm that specializes in providing investors with extensive investment research tools and resources, making it a great choice for those who want to conduct in-depth research before making investment decisions.

2. TD Ameritrade: TD Ameritrade is a brokerage firm that provides a user-friendly platform for beginners new to investing. The platform offers educational resources and tools to help users learn the basics of investing and make informed

decisions.

3. Charles Schwab: Charles Schwab is a brokerage firm known for its excellent customer service. They offer personalized support and assistance to their clients, making it an excellent choice for investors who value customer service.

4. Robinhood: Robinhood is a brokerage firm that provides a seamless digital user experience. Their app is easy to use and offers commission-free trades, making it a great choice for those prioritizing a modern and convenient user experience.

5. E-Trade: E-Trade is a brokerage firm specializing in providing ongoing education to investors. They offer various educational resources and tools to help investors stay up-to-date on the latest trends and make informed investment decisions.

6. Vanguard: Vanguard is a full-service brokerage firm specializing in low-cost index funds and ETFs. They are known for their focus on long-term investing and passive investing strategies.

These are just a few of the best brokers for investors, but it's essential to research and compare brokers to find the one that best fits your investment goals and needs.

## Investing in the Stock Market

Investing in the stock market is a powerful way to unlock a world of financial opportunity. It provides a number of advantages that can aid in wealth accumulation, long-term financial success, and future financial security.

First and foremost, investing in the stock market can generate significant returns on your investment. While there is always some risk involved, history has shown that the stock market has consistently outperformed other asset classes like bonds and cash over the long term. By investing in a diverse range of stocks, you can take advantage of the growth potential of some of the world's most successful companies and benefit from their ongoing success.

In addition to the potential for high returns, investing in the stock market can also help you to hedge against inflation. Over time, inflation can erode the value of your savings and reduce your purchasing power. But by investing in stocks, you can benefit from the rising prices of goods and services as companies grow and expand their operations.

Another key benefit of investing in the stock market is diversifying your portfolio. Investing in various stocks across different industries and sectors can spread your risk and reduce exposure to any particular company or sector. This can help you weather any market downturns and ensure your investments remain stable over the long term.

Finally, investing in the stock market can also give you a sense of control over your financial future. Unlike other investment options, such as savings accounts or bonds, investing in stocks allows you to actively manage your investments and make strategic decisions based on your financial goals and risk tolerance. This can be empowering and help you to feel more confident about your financial future.

Investing in the stock market offers a range of compelling benefits that can help you grow your wealth, hedge against inflation, diversify your portfolio, and take control of your financial future. By researching, investing wisely, and staying focused on your long-term goals, you can enjoy the many rewards the stock market offers.

The benefits of investing are far too great to pass up. Whether you're looking to create passive income, save for retirement, or build generational wealth, investing is the best way to ensure you reach your financial goals.

## Stocks and Bonds

You should be aware of many different investment types before investing your money. For now, we will focus on the three most common types of investments for new investors.

## How do stocks work

A stock can be considered a small piece of a company that an investor can purchase. When you purchase an individual stock, you become a "partial owner" of the company.

## How You Make Money

Investing in the stock market is a way to build wealth and earn passive income over time (Guglielmetti, 2021). When the company grows in value, the value of your stocks grows as well. The stock market grows about 8% annually, but investing in hand-selected individual companies can achieve much higher returns.

## How do Bonds Work

Bonds can be a smart choice for those who want to minimize risks and earn a modest return. Instead of purchasing ownership in a company, bonds allow you to lend money to the government or a corporation in exchange for regular interest payments. These investments are considered low-risk because the borrower promises to repay the borrowed amount and interest. Bond returns typically range from 2–3% per year, which may not seem impressive compared to the potential returns of the stock market. However, bonds can be valuable for those nearing retirement or looking to balance their portfolios with safer investments.

It's essential to remember that bond returns may not keep up with inflation, which is around 3% per year. However, bonds can still provide a valuable cushion against market volatility and help you diversify your investments. For example, during a stock market downturn, bond prices remain stable, providing a haven for investors. Additionally, bond returns are relatively predictable, so they can be a valuable tool for meeting short-term financial goals or for those needing a consistent income stream.

Investing in bonds can also be a socially responsible choice. Many bond offerings specifically target funding initiatives such as renewable energy projects, affordable housing, and education. By investing in these bonds, you're not only earning a return on your investment, but you're also supporting positive social change.

Bond investments may not offer the same high returns as stocks, but they can still be valuable to your investment portfolio. Their low-risk nature and predictable returns make them attractive for those seeking to minimize risks and balance their portfolios. Additionally, investing in bonds can be a socially responsible choice, allowing you to support positive initiatives while earning a return on your investment. So, consider adding bonds to your investment strategy and enjoy the benefits of stable returns and a more diverse portfolio.

# Investor Psychology

Understanding investor psychology is crucial to successful investing. Emotions play a significant role in the stock market, and knowing how they can affect your decisions is vital to making sound investment choices.

One important concept to understand is the Law of Cycles. Everything in the universe has a life cycle, from products to emotions. Understanding this law can help investors deal with the inevitable endings, whether the end of a product's life cycle or an investor's life.

By recognizing that everything is a form of energy and falls within the domain of the Law of Cycles, investors can apply good timing to their investment decisions. Like the sunrise, sunset, tides, and four seasons reflect this law, so do the stock market cycles.

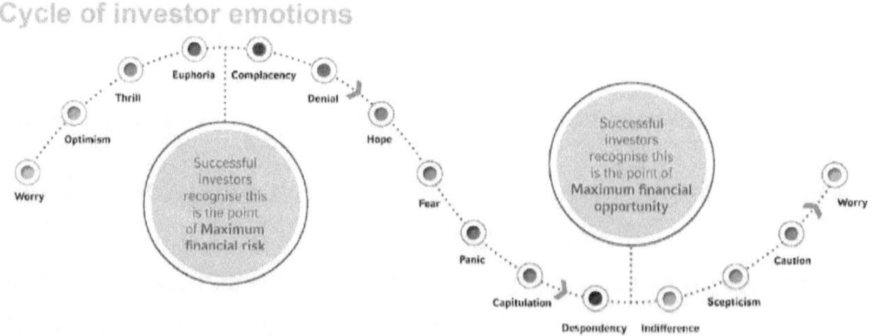


*Figure 5: Cycle of Investor Emotions*

Investors must also understand the cyclical nature of their emotions. Emotions can move from optimism to euphoria and then back down to anxiety, panic, and even depression. It's crucial to recognize when emotions are driving investment decisions and to take a step back and assess the situation objectively.

A hybrid approach to investing can help investors navigate the emotional rollercoaster of the stock market. By combining a buy-and-hold strategy with an understanding of fundamental and technical analysis, investors can make informed decisions based on data rather than emotions.

Understanding investor psychology is essential to successful investing. By recognizing the cyclical nature of products, emotions, and the stock market, investors can apply good timing and make informed decisions based on data rather than emotions. A hybrid approach to investing can help investors navigate the ups and downs of the stock market and achieve their investment goals. This cycle of emotions experienced as a stock market investor can move from optimism to pure euphoria and back down from anxiety to panic and depression.

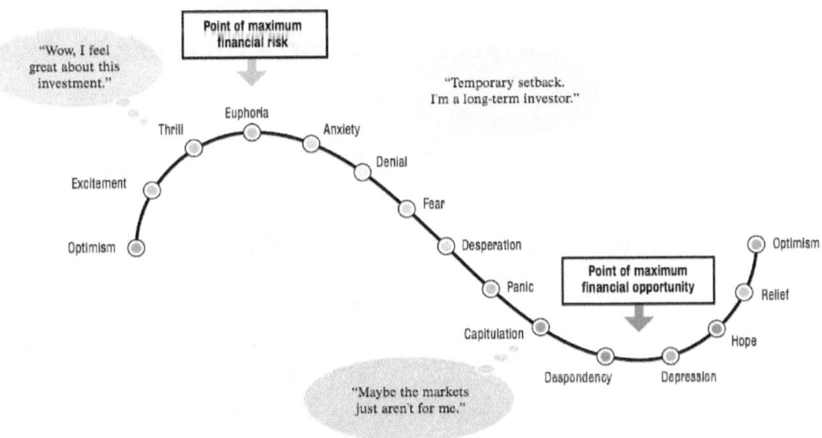


*Figure 6 Source: Russell Investments*

## Income from Dividends

Companies provide their shareholders dividends as a way to share their profits. Each share of stock you possess in the company entitles you to a certain dividend payment when the company pays out dividends. Cash, more shares of stock, or even warrants to purchase stock can all be considered dividends.

Both private and public businesses pay dividends, but not all of them do, and there is no legal need for them to do so. Dividends can be distributed monthly, quarterly, or annually if a corporation choose to pay them. Special payouts are distributed sporadically.

Not all shareholders can get dividends equally, even among corporations that do so. Several types of stock, including preferred and regular stock, generally generate different dividends or none at all. In general, preferred stock has a stronger claim to dividends than common stock, for example.

## The market is like a large pizza. How do these 11 slices of the market work?

You should diversify your portfolio widely if you plan to invest in stocks. You'll need to have shares in businesses operating in many sectors of the economy. The economy can be divided into sectors, which compile stocks with comparable commercial features. The market is divided into 11 sectors by the Global Industry Classification Standard (GICS), which includes 69 industries and 24 industry groupings. The widely accepted system influences how mutual funds and ETFs are created.

The GICS system serves as the framework for categorizing and segmenting businesses. The number of sector-based index funds that are produced and the companies included in and omitted from each index are ultimately influenced by this division. That choice is influenced by the classification scheme. Two financial sector titans, MSCI and Standard & Poor's, created GICS in 1999.

According to The Conservative Investor Daily, the classification method gets more specific and divides things into the decreasing groupings that are shown below (The Conservative Investor Daily):

1. Sectors

2. Industry groups

3. Industries

4. Sub-industries

The GICS system is occasionally updated, according to The Conservative Investor Daily, particularly when sectors expand and advance. For instance, the most recent addition to the classification is real estate. In 2016, real estate firms and REITs were separated into their own industry from the financial sector. The decision was made as a result of real estate's expanding relevance and growth, particularly equity REITs (The Conservative Investor Daily).

The reclassification had a significant impact on the sector, drawing additional capital to the stocks of those companies and recognizing the real estate sector's growth as more than merely a financial actor. To match the new weightings in the sector index, large fund companies that handled index-based funds had to purchase more of these real estate equities.

The addition or deletion of a corporation from the schema or revisions to the GICS categorization are therefore significant events. The action may change the company's ability to obtain more affordable financing and result in considerable purchasing or selling of the affected stocks.

The Industry Classification Benchmark, sometimes known as the ICB, is an alternative to the GICS schema. The market is split into 11 industries, 20 super sectors, and then even more sectors and subsectors according to the ICB, which was created in 2005 by Dow Jones and FTSE. The NASDAQ, NYSE, and other international markets currently use it.

## Understanding the 11 sectors of the stock market

The stock market is often classified into 11 sectors, each of which includes businesses engaged in a certain sector of the economy. These sectors are grouped based on the Global Industrial Classification Standard (GICS) created by Standard & Poors and MSCI. These are the 11 sectors:

1. Energy: Businesses engaged in the production and delivery of energy, such as oil and gas exploration, drilling, and refining, are included in this sector.

2. Materials: Firms engaged in the extraction and processing of raw materials, such as metals, chemicals, and paper, are included in this industry.

3. Industrials: This industry consists of businesses that produce and sell industrial goods like machinery, aerospace and military, and building materials.

4. Consumer Discretionary: This industry is made up of businesses that create products and services that aren't necessary, yet customers nonetheless want, such clothing, cars, and

entertainment.

1.  Consumer Staples: This industry comprises businesses that manufacture consumer necessities, such as food, drinks, and household goods.

2.  Health Care: This industry consists of businesses that offer pharmaceuticals, medical supplies, and healthcare facilities as well as other healthcare-related goods and services.

3.  Financials: This industry consists of businesses that offer financial services like investment management, insurance, and banking.

4.  Information Technology: This industry group consists of businesses engaged in the design, manufacture, and distribution of hardware, software, and telecommunications-related goods and services.

5.  Communication Services: This industry encompasses businesses that offer communication services, including media and telecommunications firms.

6.  Real estate: Businesses that own, develop, and manage real estate properties, including office buildings, apartments, and retail spaces, are included in this industry.Understanding the

7.  Utilities: Firms in this industry offer vital public services like electricity, water, and natural gas.

Stock market sectors is important for investors because it allows them to diversify their portfolios and gain exposure to various industries. It also helps them identify opportunities and risks associated with specific sectors and make informed investment decisions based on risk tolerance and objectives. Investors can use various financial tools and resources, such as sector-specific ETFs, mutual funds, and financial news outlets, to monitor and analyze the performance of the different sectors in the stock market.

Also, it's crucial to keep in mind that larger corporations frequently operate in many markets or industries. Even though a company may be categorized in one field, it frequently conducts substantial business in another. So, looking at what a company does can be helpful rather than being overly focused on the classification.

## Why are Electronic Traded Funds (ETF) so Powerful—also called Mutual Funds?

You would own ETF if you combined stock trading with the mutual funds' benefits of diversification. The advantages of two well-known assets are best offered through exchange-traded funds: They imitate the simplicity of trading equities while offering mutual funds benefits of diversification.

Mutual funds are a "basket of stocks" diversifying your investment over multiple companies and industries. If you have a 401k, you're most likely invested in an index or mutual fund. How You Make Money: By spreading their money in 100+ stocks at once, mutual fund investors assume that they'll make money as long as the most stocks in the group do well. The problem is that it is tough to beat the market, and you often have no idea what you're invested in.

## What is an Exchange-Traded Fund (ETF)?

An exchange-traded fund, or ETF, is a collection of investments, such as stocks or bonds. Exchange-traded funds (ETFs) allow you to invest in a variety of assets at once and usually have lower fees than other types of funds. ETF trading is also easier.

But, like any other financial instrument, ETFs are not a universally applicable solution. Take into account their merits, including management costs, commission costs (if any), simplicity of buy or sale, compatibility with your current portfolio, and investment quality.

## How do ETFs work?

Exchange-traded funds operate in the manner described below: The fund management establishes a fund to track the performance of the underlying assets, retains those assets, and then sells shares of that fund to investors. Shareholders do not own the underlying assets of an ETF; rather, they own a portion of the ETF. But, investors in an ETF that tracks a stock index may get one-time dividend payments or reinvestments for the stocks that make up the index.

ETFs, on the other hand, are made to mimic the value of an index or an underlying asset. This could also refer to a commodity like gold or a collection of stocks like the S&P 500; these trade at prices set by the market, which are typically different from those of the asset. Also, an ETF's longer-term returns will differ from those of its underlying asset due to expenditures.

## ETF Summary

Consider purchasing an ETF when you know which stocks to hold but are aware that a specific category could increase.

- An ETF provider develops many of them with a distinctive ticker after taking into account the entire universe of assets, including stocks, bonds, commodities, or currencies.

- Just like purchasing shares of a firm, investors can purchase a share of that basket.

- The ETF is traded on an exchange throughout the day, just like stocks.

## Index Funds

- Buffett (92) explained how he had instructed trustees to handle the funds he would be leaving to his wife: "Put 90% in a very low-cost S&P 500 index fund and 10% in short-term government bonds. Nov 24, 2020

- According to the investment business, the S&P 500 has performed somewhat better than the historical 10-year average between 2010 and 2020, with an average yearly return of 13.6% over the previous ten years.

- U.S. stock returns over the past 140 years have been 9.2% on average, according to Goldman Sachs. The 1930s had the worst average annual return (-4%), while the 1950s had the best average annual return (21%) of any decade.

## How do REITs work

Real Estate Investment Trusts are referred to as REITs. They were established by Congress in 1960 to provide investors with a means of profiting from real estate investments that generate income. REITs enable anyone to own or finance properties while investing in other businesses by allowing the purchase of stock. Shareholders gain from owning equities in other companies in a similar manner. Without having to go out and purchase or obtain financing for a property, the investors of a REIT receive a portion of the revenue generated by real estate investment.

Because they are required to pay shareholders taxable dividends of at least 90% of their annual taxable income, REITs can be profitable investments. In other words, a REIT is unable to keep its profits. Like a mutual fund, a REIT obtains a dividends-paid deduction, thus no tax is paid at the entity level if 100 percent of revenue is dispersed. Dividends paid to REIT shareholders are taxed at standard rates rather than the lower qualifying rate.

## Types of Traders

Different traders adopt varying strategies and time horizons when trading in financial markets. Understanding the differences between these traders can help you identify which approach may suit your goals and temperament.

Firstly, day traders aim to make quick profits by executing multiple trades daily. This requires them to closely monitor the markets and take advantage of small price movements. Day traders do not hold any trades overnight, aiming to close all positions before the market closes. This approach can be high-risk and requires a lot of skill, discipline, and mental fortitude.

On the other hand, swing traders adopt a medium-term trading strategy, holding positions for weeks, months, or even longer. They use technical and fundamental analysis to identify potential trading opportunities and usually have a higher risk tolerance than day traders. Swing traders may look for price patterns or trends and wait for an opportune moment to enter or exit a position.

Finally, positional traders have a long-term strategy, with positions held for months to years. They may use fundamental analysis to identify companies with strong growth potential or invest in a diversified portfolio of stocks. Positional traders aim to capture the market's long-term trend and may not be as concerned about short-term price movements. This approach requires patience, discipline, and a long-term perspective.

Whether you are a day trader, swing trader, or positional trader, you must have a well-defined strategy that suits your goals, temperament, and risk tolerance. Understanding the differences between these approaches can help you make informed decisions and increase your chances of success in the markets.

## Swing Trading

The room was filled with the muted sounds of keyboards clacking and traders speaking into headsets as Kevin sat intently at his desk, eyes fixed on the charts before him. He had been swing trading in the stock market for years, but this week had been unlike any other. As a swing trader, he buys and sells financial securities, such as stocks or currencies, to profit from short-term price fluctuations.

It had started with a risky move, buying up shares of a pharmaceutical company still in its early stages of development. The stock had been volatile, but Kevin had a hunch that it was about to take off. Swing traders often use technical analysis to identify potential entry and exit points for their trades, and they may employ a variety of strategies to manage risk and maximize profits. He had poured a portion of his resources into it, risking much of his entire portfolio on this one move. At first, it seemed like it might not pay off. The stock wavered, dipping and rising but never hitting the level Kevin had hoped for. But he refused to give up. He continued to watch the charts, studying the patterns and the data, looking for any signs of a breakthrough. And then, on the third day, it happened. The stock suddenly shot up, rising far beyond what Kevin had expected. He watched with awe and disbelief as his investment grew exponentially, the numbers on the screen soaring higher and higher.

It was a moment of triumph, a vindication of his trading skills and instincts. But it was also a reminder of the risks and rewards of the stock market, a world of uncertainty and possibility that could change on a dime.

For Kevin, it was a lesson that he would carry with him always. A reminder that sometimes, the biggest risks were the ones that paid off the most and that the key to success in the stock market was to keep a steady hand, a clear mind, and a willingness to take bold chances when the opportunity presented itself.

As the day ended, Kevin leaned back in his chair and smiled. He had made a fortune and in doing so, had proven that he was a master of the stock market, a player to be reckoned with in a world of risk and reward. The adventure was the beginning for him, and he couldn't wait to see where it would take him next.

## Trend Trading

The name itself conjures images of successful traders making a fortune in the markets. And it's not just a daydream; trend trading can be an excellent part-time business for anyone looking to supplement their income. Here's why:

First and foremost, trend trading allows you to capitalize on the market's overall direction. You don't have to fret over every little price movement. Trend trading lets you take a more laid-back approach to the markets. It's a far less stressful and time-consuming way to trade, letting you focus on your other commitments.

Plus, trend trading is perfect for anyone who wants to balance trading with other aspects of their life. Many trend traders only need to spend a few hours per week analyzing the market and placing trades. It's an excellent option for those who want to keep their day job but still make some extra cash.

And speaking of cash, trend trading can be incredibly lucrative. As you follow the trends, you can make significant profits over time. With time-tested trading rules and a little bit of patience, our members have reported impressive trading profits. Who knows? You could be the next success story.

But what if you're new to trading? No problem! Trend trading is relatively easy to learn, and plenty of resources are available to help you get started. On our website, we offer comprehensive guides to trend trading, with a variety of strategies to suit different traders' needs.

Overall, trend trading is a great choice for anyone looking for a flexible, profitable part-time business. With the right approach, you can build your trading skills and start seeing results quickly. So why wait? Trend trading could be your perfect side business if you're interested in the markets and want to boost your income.

## Position trading

Position trading has a long-term trading strategy in which an investor buys and holds a financial security, such as a stock or a currency, for an extended period, typically several months or years.

Position traders seek to profit from the fundamental growth and appreciation of the underlying asset rather than trying to capture short-term price fluctuations. They typically use fundamental analysis to identify strong companies or markets with a favorable long-term outlook and then buy and hold the asset until it reaches its target price or until the investor's investment objectives change.

Position traders may also use technical analysis to help identify entry and exit points for their trades. Still, their focus is on identifying the asset's underlying value and holding it for the long term. This strategy requires patience, discipline, and the ability to tolerate short-term volatility and market fluctuations.

Position trading can be a good option for investors who are looking for a more passive, hands-off approach to investing, as it requires less monitoring and trading activity than other short-term strategies. Position traders conduct thorough research and analysis before making any investment. They also:

- Know the current market conditions. Understand the direction of the trend.

- Keep a trading journal to have a feedback loop for tracking progress

- Place stop-loss orders to cut their losses short let your runners run.

- Use a 3:1 or greater reward-to-risk ratio

- Avoid buying any stocks that are below over 200-day moving average

- Are not afraid to trade options

## Your stock portfolio's ultimate goal

Your stock portfolio is your key to unlocking a world of financial opportunity. With a carefully curated selection of high-quality companies, you can generate income, hedge your portfolio, and increase your stake in the best businesses. But your ultimate goal is so much more than just making a quick buck. You're building a stable source of income for your retirement, protected against the ravages of inflation. And you're doing it by investing in companies that offer rock-solid compounding dividend growth and long-term capital gains. These investments will set you up for financial success for years to come.

## Trading versus Investing

When comparing fundamental and technical research, it is important to understand the key differences between investors and traders. While traders prioritize fast income or aggressive account growth, investors are more interested in long-term growth. Market participants frequently favor one strategy over the other. But a lot of people combine the two.

Becoming an expert in any field, much less both, can be difficult because investing and trading are two very different worlds. Knowing which style, to what extent, and for what reasons will depend on your timetable is crucial.

Investing and trading are two different approaches to making money in the financial markets. Investing involves buying and holding assets with the goal of generating returns over a longer time frame, typically several years or more. Trading, on the other hand, involves buying and selling assets to make profits in the short term, usually within days, weeks, or months.

The key difference between investing and trading is the time frame of the transactions. Investors generally take a long-term view of the market and are willing to hold onto their assets through ups and downs, with the expectation that they will appreciate in value over time. They typically focus on the underlying fundamentals of the assets they invest in, such as a company's financial health, management team, and industry trends.

On the other hand, traders are more focused on short-term price movements and use technical analysis and other tools to identify trading opportunities. They aim to profit from market volatility and may take advantage of both rising and falling prices.

Another important difference between investing and trading is the level of risk involved. Investing is generally considered less risky than trading, as investors have a longer time horizon and are less susceptible to short-term market fluctuations. However, investing still involves some level of risk, as the value of assets can fluctuate over time and may be affected by factors such as economic conditions, interest rates, and geopolitical events.

In contrast, trading is generally considered more risky than investing, as traders are exposed to short-term market volatility and may be subject to higher transaction costs, such as brokerage fees and taxes.

Overall, investing and trading are two different approaches to making money in the financial markets, each with its own advantages and risks. The choice between the two will depend on a range of factors, including an investor's financial goals, risk tolerance, and time horizon.

Here are some advantages and risks associated with investing and trading:

## Advantages of Investing:

1. Potential for long-term returns: Investing in assets such as stocks, bonds, or real estate can provide the potential for significant long-term returns if the assets appreciate in value over time.

2. Passive income: Many investments, such as dividend-paying stocks, can provide a steady stream of passive income over time.

3. Diversification: Investing across a range of asset classes and industries can help to spread risk and reduce the impact of market volatility.

4. Lower transaction costs: Compared to trading, investing typically involves lower transaction costs, such as brokerage fees and taxes.

## Risks of Investing:

1. Market volatility: The value of investments can fluctuate over time, and investors may experience losses during periods of market volatility.

2. Long-term horizon: Investing typically requires a longer time horizon than trading, and investors may need to be patient in order to see significant returns.

3. Inflation: Inflation can erode the value of investments over time, particularly if the returns fail to keep pace with inflation.

## Advantages of Trading:

1. Potential for short-term profits: Traders can profit from short-

term price movements in the markets, and may be able to generate significant returns in a short period of time.

2. Flexibility: Trading allows investors to respond quickly to market conditions and adjust their positions accordingly.

3. High liquidity: Traders can buy and sell assets quickly and easily, with no long-term commitment required.

4. Short-term horizon: Trading typically involves a shorter time horizon than investing, which can allow traders to take advantage of more immediate opportunities.

## Risks of Trading:

1. Market volatility: Traders are exposed to short-term market fluctuations, which can result in significant losses if the market moves against their positions.

2. High transaction costs: Trading can involve higher transaction costs than investing, including brokerage fees, commissions, and taxes.

3. Emotional decisions: Traders may be more susceptible to making emotional decisions based on short-term market movements, rather than sticking to a longer-term investment strategy.

4. Need for specialized knowledge: Successful trading requires a high level of specialized knowledge, including technical analysis and market research.

Overall, both investing and trading involve risks and potential rewards, and the choice between the two will depend on an investor's financial goals, risk tolerance, and time horizon. It's important for investors to carefully consider these factors before making any investment decisions.

## Technical analysis

Technicians study price patterns. Technical analysis examines a security's price movement and makes predictions about future price changes using this information. Generally speaking, the price patterns on the chart are more trustworthy the more liquid the product. A high-volume index product, such as the SPY ETF, will produce more trustworthy investor and trader sentiment on the charts than a penny stock with little trading activity.

In addition to selecting from among thousands of "indicators" and combinations, technicians frequently focus on chart price activity. Hardcore geek techs have said things like, "This indication (or collection of indicators) works with technical analysis," countless times, and I can't count. We might concentrate on price action to gain a competitive edge in the markets. As investors, the growth of our accounts is based on the appreciation of the assets we possess. In order to follow and trade in the direction of the assets we wish to possess, it only makes sense to concentrate on price charts and employ technical analysis.But the advantages of technical analysis don't stop there. Here are just a few of the benefits:

- Technical analysis works with any time frame, from minutes to months.

- It can be applied to all assets, including indexes, stocks, commodities, and currencies.

- It helps you identify low-risk, high-probability trade setups.

- You can define risk and place protective stops to minimize potential losses.

- You can define profit potential and set limit orders to lock in gains.

- Technical analysis eliminates guesswork, giving you a simple, repeatable, rule-based system for generating a reliable ROI.

- Through technical analysis, you can gain clarity on an asset's trend, ensuring you only own and hold positions in rising value assets.

With technical analysis, you can have confidence in your trading decisions, knowing you're basing them on reliable data and proven strategies. Whether you're a seasoned pro or a newbie, technical analysis can help you achieve your investment goals and build a successful portfolio market and all timeframes."

I have been trading for over 20 years and have not encountered such a thing. Be cautious of chasing after indicators you think will be the holy grail. The "forest" of indicators is vast, and it's easy to get lost. Technicians can do well with a relatively small group of indicators and patterns. Knowing when and how to apply them under different conditions is crucial.

## Fundamental analysis

Fundamental analysis evaluates the intrinsic value of a stock or security by examining its financial and economic factors. In other words, it is a way of understanding the underlying business and economic forces that affect a company's stock price. The purpose of fundamental analysis is to identify stocks that are trading at a discount to their intrinsic value and therefore have the potential to provide a good return on investment.

The fundamental analysis examines various factors, including a company's financial statements, management team, competitive position, industry trends, and economic conditions. Analyzing these factors helps an investor understand the company's current financial health and future growth prospects. Some key metrics used in fundamental analyses include earnings per share, price-to-earnings ratio, return on equity, and dividend yield.

One of the primary benefits of fundamental analysis is that it can provide a long-term perspective on a company's financial health and growth potential. This is important because the stock market is often driven by short-term fluctuations and speculation, which can create volatility and uncertainty. By focusing on the underlying fundamentals of a company, an investor can make more informed decisions about buying and holding a stock over the long term.

Fundamental analysis can also help investors identify trends and changes in the market that may affect a particular stock or sector. For example, suppose an investor is interested in the technology sector. In that case, they may use fundamental analysis to identify which companies have strong growth potential and which ones are struggling due to changes in the industry or competition from new entrants.

Another advantage of fundamental analysis is that it can help investors identify potential risks and weaknesses in a company's financial position. By understanding the underlying financial and economic factors that drive a company's stock price, investors can make more informed decisions about when to sell or avoid a particular stock.

Fundamental analysis is a valuable tool for investors making informed decisions about investing in the stock market. Investors can better understand a company's intrinsic value and growth potential by examining its financial and economic factors. While no method can predict the future with certainty, fundamental analysis can provide a solid foundation for making informed investment decisions.

## Here is why I like Technical analysis as a trader

As a technician, my opinion on what constitutes a "correct" valuation may not be as relevant as what big money thinks and how they move their capital. That's why I look to the price action from the charts to gain an edge as a technical trader. By following the money, rather than relying solely on my personal opinions about valuation, I can make high-probability entries and exits.

While fundamental analysis is certainly important, as a technician, I focus on the charts to understand what big money is doing. This means that I can potentially ignore fundamentals and still be successful in the market. After all, efficient market theory suggests that all known fundamentals are already baked into the price.

However, it's important to remember that even the most reliable chart patterns and indicators can unexpectedly fail. That's why good risk management is always a requirement. As a technician, I am always mindful of the potential risks and take steps to mitigate them.

As a technician, focusing on price action and following the money allows me to make high-probability trades in the market. While fundamentals are important, my expertise lies in reading the charts and understanding what big money is doing. By managing risk and staying focused on the charts, I can make informed trading decisions and achieve success as a technical trader.

## A hybrid approach to buy-and-hold

There are two primary schools of thought in stock picking investing: the buy-and-hold and active approaches. The buy-and-hold approach involves purchasing stocks and holding them for an extended period, often years or even decades, to take advantage of the stock's potential for growth. On the other hand, the active approach involves buying and selling stocks more frequently to try to outperform the market.

However, there is a third approach that combines the best aspects of both buy-and-hold and active investing. This is known as the hybrid approach, which involves actively managing a portfolio of stocks while holding onto them for the long term.

The hybrid approach begins with a rigorous fundamental analysis of each stock in the portfolio. This analysis includes examining the company's financial statements, earnings reports, and other vital data points to determine its overall financial health and growth potential. The goal of this analysis is to identify stocks that have strong fundamentals and a solid potential for growth.

Once the stocks have been selected, the hybrid investor will actively manage the portfolio by periodically reviewing the stocks' performance and adjusting as necessary. For example, if a stock's performance falters, the investor may sell it and replace it with another stock with better growth potential. On the other hand, if a stock is performing exceptionally well, the investor may choose to hold onto it for the long term, taking advantage of its potential for continued growth.

The key to success with a hybrid approach is to strike the right balance between active management and long-term holding. The investor must be diligent in monitoring the stocks in the portfolio and be willing to make changes when necessary. However, they must also be patient enough to hold onto stocks for the long term to take advantage of their full growth potential.

One of the benefits of the hybrid approach is that it can offer a higher potential return than a traditional buy-and-hold approach while still offering the security of long-term holding. By actively managing the portfolio, the investor can take advantage of market trends and other opportunities while still holding onto the stocks for the long term.

Investors can benefit from the best of both worlds with the hybrid approach to stock selection. By combining the rigor of fundamental analysis with the flexibility of active management, investors can earn considerable returns while retaining a long-term perspective. With careful attention and a disciplined approach, the hybrid technique can be a strong tool for investors wanting to generate wealth through stock selecting. If you're a "buy and hold" long-term investor, you might disregard technical research. But if you did, you'd be harming yourself. Why? Staying out of the markets and economy is preferable because they are cyclical to prevent dramatic declines. Furthermore, when fear and greed take control, fundamentals may be much out of step with price movement. "The Market can be crazy for as long as you can have your finances in order."

Maintaining a complete investment through significant price and economic corrections can be costly to long-term outcomes. At times, technical analysis can show buy-and-hold investors when a security has bottomed out, is oversold, and may have a good chance of re-entering the market. But once more, prudent risk management is necessary to safeguard our funds.

## Fundamental Investing vs. Technical Analysis

Which one would you prefer? It relies on what best suits your personality in addition to your time frame. I doubt that performing a fundamental investigation of a publicly traded company will allow me to notice something that few people do. I would then be a first-order participant against a horde of institutional pros with no advantage. I am a second-order technician participant. My goal is to make decisions based on an accurate assessment of the price activity.

## Critical stock trading rules to follow

As a savvy stock trader, there's no denying the importance of having a set of critical rules to live by. Sticking to these essential principles could make or break your success in the market. Here are ten guidelines to follow to ensure you're on the right track

1.  Review the stock market conditions and significant news before trading. This will give you an accurate sense of the overall landscape and potential opportunities.

2.  Watch how the market opens for the first 30 minutes of the trading day. This can be a critical time for making informed trading decisions.

3.  Focus on the strongest companies in the best sectors when buying stocks. This will ensure that your investments have the greatest potential for long-term success

4.  Use limit orders to orders to buy and sell stocks as much as possible. This tactic can help you get the best price for your trades.

5.  Set a stop loss of 7-10% for each trade and limit total risk on

any single trade to less than 5%.

6.  Avoid purchasing low-volume stocks, which can be challenging to buy and sell at the right time.

7.  Cut your losses early and let yhour winners ride. This strategy can help you maximize returns and minimize losses

8.  Have a plan for the stocks you purchase and stick to it. This will help you make informed decisions and achieve your long-term financial goals

9.  Keep a notebook to track progress, what worked and what did not work. This will help you track your successes and failures and learn from them.

10. Consider diversifying your trades among the top-performing sectors.

Following these ten essential stock trading rules can help you succeed. By being diligent, strategic, and mindful of risks, you can make informed decisions and achieve your long-term financial goals.

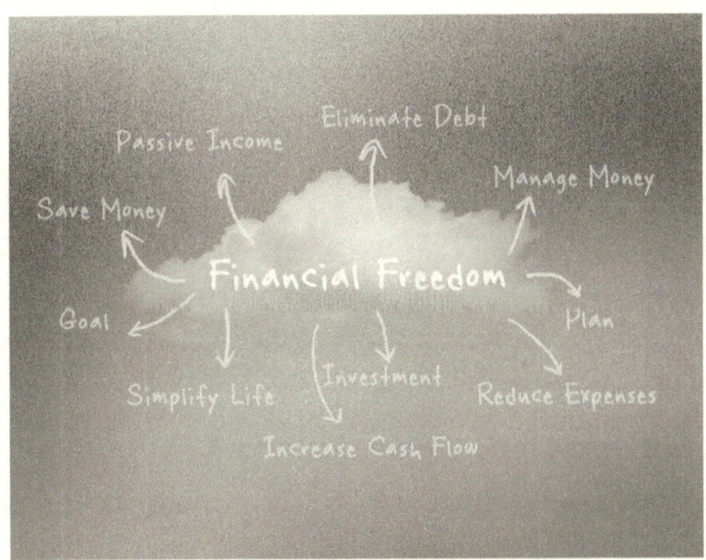

# CHAPTER 7: FINANCIAL STATEMENTS THAT MATTER

## UNDERSTANDING THE BASICS FOR LONG-TERM GROWTH

"Understanding financial statements is essential for investors who want to make informed decisions and achieve long-term growth. By analyzing key financial metrics, investors can gain a deeper understanding of a company's financial health and make more strategic investment decisions." — *Warren Buffett*

Financial statements are documents made to provide investors with an overview of a company's performance over time. Before purchasing a stock, investors should consider several factors, including the following.

1. How does the company generate revenue?

2. Have sales and profits increased or decreased for the company?

3.  How much property does the company own?

4.  How much debt does the company have?

5.  Is more money flowing in or leaving the country?

## How to Find a Company's Financial Statements

An aspiring investor named Sarah dreamed of building a long-term investment portfolio to provide her with financial freedom. However, she didn't know where to start and felt overwhelmed by the complex financial jargon.

She once ran across a wealthy investor who introduced her to the income statement, balance sheet, and statement of cash flows—the three key financial statements. He explained that she could gain insights into a business's financial health and make informed investment decisions by understanding these statements.

Sarah eagerly took up the challenge and started learning about these financial statements. She discovered that the income statement summarized a company's revenues and expenses, revealing its profitability over a specific period. On the other hand, the balance sheet gave her a snapshot of a company's financial position, including its assets, liabilities, and equity. Finally, the statement of cash flows provided insights into a company's cash flow activities, which helped her determine its ability to generate cash and manage its finances.

As Sarah continued to study and apply what she had learned, she became more confident in her investment decisions. She identified businesses with strong financial positions, solid revenues, and consistent cash flow management and invested in them with the knowledge that they had a high potential for long-term growth.

In the end, Sarah's hard work and dedication paid off. Her investment portfolio grew steadily, and she achieved her dream of financial freedom. She realized that understanding the three most important financial statements was critical for investing and empowering her personal life. She could now make informed financial decisions that would benefit her for years.

Financial statements for a corporation are available directly from the business. The most recent quarterly earnings report should be located on the company's investor relations (IR) page, typically under the "news," "press releases," or "financials" tabs at the top of the page. Many corporations on their primary IR page keep their most recent results in the spotlight. For instance, a news release containing Apple's most recent financial results is the top item on the company's investor relations page. There is a link to the consolidated financial statements, which include the three key papers covered above, directly on the news release.

Undoubtedly, there are other ways to locate a company's financial statements. For instance, you can check out the business's most recent quarterly report on the SEC website. The financial statements may also be accessible through your brokerage's stock quotes, which is a simple way to obtain them.

The bottom line is that financial statements for all publicly traded firms listed on significant U.S. exchanges are comprehensive, updated quarterly, and easily accessible to assist investors like you in making informed judgments.

## The Income Statement

The income statement of a business reveals the amount of revenue it received and the amount of profit (ideally) it generated from that revenue. It starts with the business's sales and demonstrates how it converts them into profit.

The sum "top-line": The top-line figure, usually referred to as net sales or revenues, is the first important figure on the income statement. A company's financial statement frequently delineates its many revenue streams.

Earnings (net income): The business's gross income is then calculated after deducting its cost of sales. Its operating income is calculated after deducting operating expenses (such as those for research & development). The business's net income, commonly referred to as its "earnings," is then obtained by deducting income tax expenses. One big number and shares are frequently used to represent net income (the latter being earnings per share or EPS).

The income statement may also include other data, such as sales broken down by area or product category, depending on the business. It's also important to note that an income statement often has numerous columns of numbers that compare the current period to the same period last year. The most recent quarter and the company's year-to-date (or full year) will often be contrasted with the same quarters from the previous year. The present income of the company and the prior year's income demonstrate how the business is expanding.

**Example Corporation**
**Income Statement**
**Years ended December 31**

(in thousands of dollars)

| | 2022 | 2021 | 2020 |
|---|---|---|---|
| Net sales | $ 3,980 | $ 3,750 | $ 3,400 |
| Cost of sales | 3,100 | 2,950 | 2,700 |
| Gross profit | 880 | 800 | 700 |
| Selling, general and administrative expenses | 640 | 590 | 510 |
| Operating income | 240 | 210 | 190 |
| Interest expense | 20 | 15 | 15 |
| Loss on sale of equipment | 5 | - | 4 |
| Income before income taxes | 215 | 195 | 171 |
| Income tax expense | 50 | 40 | 36 |
| Net income | $ 165 | $ 155 | $ 135 |

See notes to the financial statements.

*Figure 7*

## The Balance Sheet

A company's balance sheet provides a snapshot of its financial situation at any one time (typically at the end of a quarter). The data is often given as a comparison between the current period and the same time last year, just like the income statement.

A balance sheet is divided into three sections:

1.  Assets: The things the business possesses. Other divisions include current assets and noncurrent assets. Assets that can be projected to become liquid within a year are included in current assets. Cash, short-term treasuries, accounts receivable, and inventories are a few examples. Long-term investments, real estate, and manufacturing equipment are just a few examples of noncurrent assets.

2. Liabilities: are debts owed by the business. There are two categories for these: current and noncurrent. The payments a business must make within a year, such as accounts payable and short-term debt, are included in current liabilities. Long-term debts are among the noncurrent liabilities.

3. Shareholder's equity: Picture shareholder's equity as the amount of money the business would have left over after liquidating all of its assets and paying off all of its debts. The difference between assets and liabilities, or shareholder equity, represents the company's net value.

**Example Corporation**
**Balance Sheet**
**December 31, 2022**

| ASSETS | | LIABILITIES | |
|---|---|---|---|
| Current assets | | Current liabilities | |
| Cash and cash equivalents | $ 2,200 | Short-term loans payable | $ 5,000 |
| Short-term investments | 10,000 | Current portion of long-term debt | 15,000 |
| Accounts receivable - net | 39,500 | Accounts payable | 20,900 |
| Other receivables | 1,000 | Accrued compensation and benefits | 8,500 |
| Inventory | 31,000 | Income taxes payable | 6,100 |
| Supplies | 3,800 | Other accrued liabilities | 4,000 |
| Prepaid expenses | 1,500 | Deferred revenues | 1,500 |
| Total current assets | 89,000 | Total current liabilities | 61,000 |
| | | | |
| Investments | 36,000 | Long-term liabilities | |
| | | Notes payable | 20,000 |
| Property, plant & equipment - net | | Bonds payable | 375,000 |
| Land | 5,500 | Deferred income taxes | 25,000 |
| Land improvements | 6,500 | Total long-term liabilities | 420,000 |
| Buildings | 180,000 | | |
| Equipment | 201,000 | Total liabilities | 481,000 |
| Less: accumulated depreciation | (56,000) | | |
| Property, plant & equipment - net | 337,000 | Commitments and contingencies (see notes) | |
| | | | |
| Intangible assets | | STOCKHOLDERS' EQUITY | |
| Goodwill | 105,000 | | |
| Other intangible assets | 200,000 | Common stock | 110,000 |
| Total intangible assets | 305,000 | Retained earnings | 220,000 |
| | | Accum other comprehensive income | 9,000 |
| Other assets | 3,000 | Less: Treasury stock | (50,000) |
| | | Total stockholders' equity | 289,000 |
| Total assets | $ 770,000 | Total liabilities & stockholders' equity | $ 770,000 |

*The accompanying notes are an integral part of this statement.*

*Figure 8*

## The Cash Flow statement

The cash flow statement displays the money coming into and going out of a company. This is divided into the following three groups:

1. Operational activities: They consist of the company's net income from operations, stock-based compensation, collected receivables, paid accounts payable, and other business-related items.

2. Investment activities: This section of the cash flow statement includes any stock or bond purchases or sales made by the company. The same holds true whether the company buys or sells property or machinery.

3. Financing activities: This section of the cash flow statement includes any new common stock that a company issues. Both dividend payments and stock buybacks are frequent outflows in this segment. Moreover, a line item will be added here if a business pays off debt.

The sum of these categories is the company's cash flow. A positive number demonstrates that the company's cash flow improved throughout the time period, whilst a negative number reveals a decline. A total of the company's current cash and cash equivalents will appear just under the cash flow figure.

<table>
<tr><td colspan="2" align="center">Example Corporation<br>Statement of Cash Flows<br>For the year ended December 31, 2022</td></tr>
<tr><td>Cash flows from operating activities</td><td align="right">$230,000</td></tr>
<tr><td>Net income</td><td></td></tr>
<tr><td>Adjustments to reconcile net income to net cash<br>  provided by operating activities:</td><td></td></tr>
<tr><td>Depreciation and amortization</td><td align="right">63,000</td></tr>
<tr><td>Loss on sale of equipment</td><td align="right">15,000</td></tr>
<tr><td>Changes in current assets and liabilities:</td><td></td></tr>
<tr><td>  Increase in accounts receivable</td><td align="right">(21,000)</td></tr>
<tr><td>  Decrease in prepaid expenses</td><td align="right">3,000</td></tr>
<tr><td>  Decrease in accounts payable</td><td align="right">(28,000)</td></tr>
<tr><td>Net cash provided by operating activities</td><td align="right">262,000</td></tr>
<tr><td></td><td></td></tr>
<tr><td>Cash flows from investing activities</td><td></td></tr>
<tr><td>  Capital expenditures</td><td align="right">(300,000)</td></tr>
<tr><td>  Proceeds from sale of equipment</td><td align="right">40,000</td></tr>
<tr><td>Net cash used for investing activities</td><td align="right">(260,000)</td></tr>
<tr><td></td><td></td></tr>
<tr><td>Cash flows from financing activities</td><td></td></tr>
<tr><td>  Proceeds from issuing debt</td><td align="right">200,000</td></tr>
<tr><td>  Dividends paid</td><td align="right">(110,000)</td></tr>
<tr><td>Net cash provided by financing activities</td><td align="right">90,000</td></tr>
<tr><td></td><td></td></tr>
<tr><td>Net increase in cash during the year</td><td align="right">92,000</td></tr>
<tr><td>Cash at the beginning of the year</td><td align="right">101,000</td></tr>
<tr><td>Cash at the end of the year</td><td align="right">$193,000</td></tr>
<tr><td colspan="2" align="center">Notes to the financial statements.</td></tr>
</table>

*Figure 9*

## What is EBITDA?

John C. Malone, the former president, and CEO of Cable and Media Behemoth Tele-Communications Inc., created the EBITDA statistic for company research in the 1970s. With this equation, you can predict a business's long-term profitability and assess its capacity to pay back future loans.

Earnings Before Interest, Taxes, Depreciation, and Amortization is referred to as EBITDA. Finding investors for businesses with long-term growth potential can be aided by the EBITDA formula, which is also a reliable approach to compare businesses.

## Top six key financial ratios to know when analyzing a stock

Financial ratios can be used to increase your understanding of a company, but you should always consider them all at once rather than concentrating on just one or two ratios. Ratio-based financial research is only one phase in the stock investment process. Research management and learn what they have to say about a company, too. Sometimes, a business's future depends primarily on factors that are difficult to measure.

1. Earnings per share (EPS)

One of the most popular ratios in the financial industry is earnings per share or EPS. This figure reveals the profit generated by a corporation for each share of stock that is currently outstanding. A company's net income is divided by the total number of outstanding shares to arrive at its earnings per share (EPS).

Here is how to calculate earnings per share: (Net Income - Preferred Dividends) / Weighted Average Number of Common Shares is the formula for calculating earnings per share.

For stock investors, understanding this ratio's boundaries is just as critical as knowing it. The many accounting procedures that might affect net income and earnings per share are mostly under the discretion of executives. Make sure you comprehend how earnings are determined rather than simply accepting EPS at face value.*2.*

2. Price/earnings ratio (P/E)

The P/E ratio, which divides a company's stock price by earnings per share, is another typical statistic. Investors use this ratio to assess how much value they are receiving in relation to the price they paid for a share of stock because it is a valuation ratio.

The P/E Ratio Formula is as follows: The equation for the P/E ratio is Share Price Earnings per Share:

Successful companies with average or below-average growth prospects typically sell at lower P/E ratios than companies with strong growth prospects. One of the most successful investors in the world, Warren Buffett, has created a fortune by purchasing shares of companies with strong growth potential and cheap P/E ratios. Both an investment in Apple (AAPL) made more recently and one in Coca-Cola (KO) made billions for Berkshire Hathaway stockholders when they were sold for low P/E ratios.

P/E ratios can be calculated using the company's projected earnings as well as its trailing earnings or earnings that have already been earned. Looking at the projected P/E ratio instead of using past earnings, which can result in an increased ratio, may be more advantageous for rapidly expanding companies. But, keep in mind that projections are not guarantees, and many stocks of businesses that were once regarded as fast-growers suffered when that growth did not occur.

To determine an earnings yield, the P/E ratio can also be reversed.

Investors can readily compare the yield to other investment opportunities by dividing profits per share by the stock price.**3.**

## 3. Price/Earnings-to-Growth or PEG Ratio

The price/earnings-to-growth (PEG) ratio, which is less well-known than its P/E counterpart, may offer an even more thorough and precise picture of a stock's future growth potential.

The PEG Ratio formula is as follows: PEG ratio = P/E ratio / EPS Growth

You may be familiar with a stock's P/E ratio, but how does that figure compare to the expected growth rate? A company's price-to-earnings ratio might be "cheap," but what good is it if the company can't manage to expand?

With this ratio, the P/E is compared to the analyst consensus estimate of predicted earnings, which can range from quarterly to five years in the future, according to Fairbourn. How, then, might you interpret this? If the PEG ratio is less than one, Fairbourn advised investors to see the stock as being cheap.

Why is the growth factor so crucial? You shouldn't invest in something that will always be a good deal, according to Fairbourn. Investors frequently demand to see past growth in addition to future growth. This might support the validity of a PEG ratio that is too low.

## 4. Price-to-Sales or P/S Ratio

Some businesses may have strong quarterly revenue (another name for "sales") but poor earnings, maybe as a result of spending a significant amount of their revenue. Some investors are ready to give up earnings today in exchange for future returns that could be far higher. They know that some businesses might have to invest their cash and quarterly sales revenues to expand and improve. Sales are what matter in this situation.

The P/S Ratio Formula is as follows: Stock Price / Sales Per Share is the P/S Ratio.

The price-to-sales (P/S) ratio reveals the premium that investors are ready to pay over a company's "revenues" (not "profits," which are gross revenues fewer liabilities).

Although revenue may not be as "solid" as earnings, utilizing revenue as the basis for valuation has some interesting advantages, as Fairbourn noted. Sales are typically less susceptible to managerial manipulation than profitability, he claimed. Alternatively said, sales are sales, period. Although different costs may have an impact on profits, a company's sales are often easy to understand.

"The P/S aids in our comprehension of the connection between a company's annual sales and its present stock price. Hence, if a ratio gives us a reading of, say, .53, it means that we are paying .53 a share for every dollar the company generates in revenue, according to Fairbourn. Does that seem like a good deal, or is that a good deal? "The P/S helps us understand the relationship between the current stock price and a company's annual sales. So, if a ratio gives us a reading of, say, .53, then the ratio tells us that we are paying 53 cents per share for every dollar the company makes in sales," Fairbourn explained. Does that sound like a bargain, or does that sound like a bargain?

5. Return on equity (ROE)

The return on equity, or the profit a firm makes using its owners' capital, is one of the most crucial statistics to comprehend. It gauges a company's effectiveness at generating additional wealth for its shareholders. If you had two businesses that made $1 million in revenue each this year, but one of them had to spend $10 million to do so. The other just only $5 million in contrast. It would be obvious that the second business did better that year.

This is the ROE proportion: Sales x Assets x Equity x Sales x Profits before taxes = ROE (1 - Tax Rate).

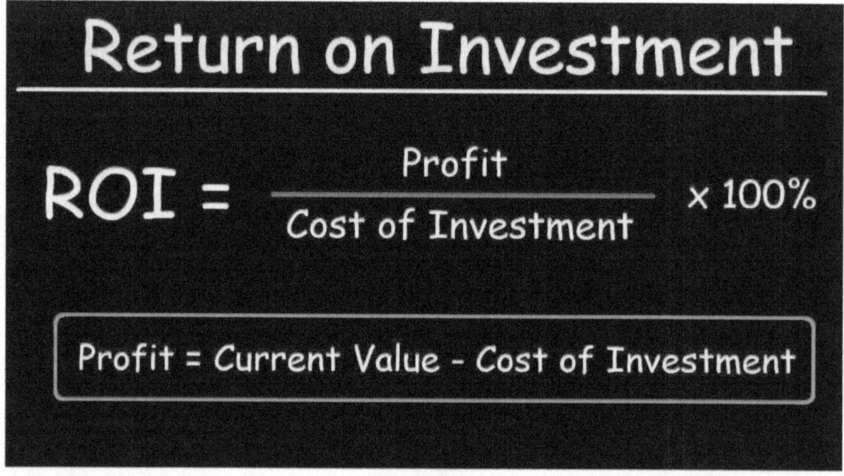


*Figure 10*

6. Debt-to-capital ratio

You should monitor a company's profitability in addition to learning how it is financed and whether it can handle its amount of debt. The debt-to-capital ratio, which adds short- and long-term debt and divides it by the company's total capital, is one approach to look at this. The higher the ratio, the more indebted a corporation is. Debt-to-capital ratios exceeding 40% typically call for a closer examination to make sure the business can manage the debt load.

The debt-to-equity ratio is calculated as follows: total liabilities / total shareholders' equity

The type of funding a business chooses will depend on its particular needs. In order to prevent potential defaults during economic downturns when sales and earnings tend to be lower, more cyclical enterprises should rely less on debt funding. On the other hand, because to their greater predictability, consistent performers in stable organizations may frequently support debt levels above the norm.

## Ratio Summary

Once you realize that evaluating a stock's worth might offer the prospective direction that aids in determining whether an opportunity is good or too risky, you can decide for yourself. These six important financial ratios ought to get you going. Remember that even while they can't tell you everything vital about a business, having a clear view of the road ahead can help you decide where to go and whether to accelerate or decelerate.

## US Gross Domestic Product (GDP)

An important indicator of productivity in the US is GDP. GDP stands for Gross Domestic Product and is the total value of all goods and services *produced* by a country in a stated period. Economists, investors, and central banks closely monitor annual and quarterly GDP estimates —primary indicators of a country's economic health.

GDP can be calculated as *nominal,* a simple period-to-period percentage change, or *real,* where this change considers the inflation rate. Real GDP is what I quoted above and is the number that matters when determining any accurate measure of activity. Most importantly, how is it changing from period to period?

What we must understand about our monetary system is that central bankers rely on several economic indicators to make major policy decisions that can affect virtually every single person living and operating within that economy.

Timely or not, GDP is a critical key indicator for the Fed and central bankers. Also, companies rely on many of the same indicators to decide on hiring and investment for their businesses. Consumers look at GDP and inflation measures, and their confidence levels affect their spending, affecting those same numbers.

As investors, we look at GDP numbers to determine whether they should buy a nation's sovereign debt. A nation with a high debt-to-GDP ratio could indicate a looming debt crisis for them. Remember, GDP is a nation's revenue.

The Gross Domestic Product (GDP) in the United States was worth 23315 billion US dollars in 2021, according to official data from the World Bank. The GDP value of the United States represents 10.41 percent of the world economy. Source: World Bank

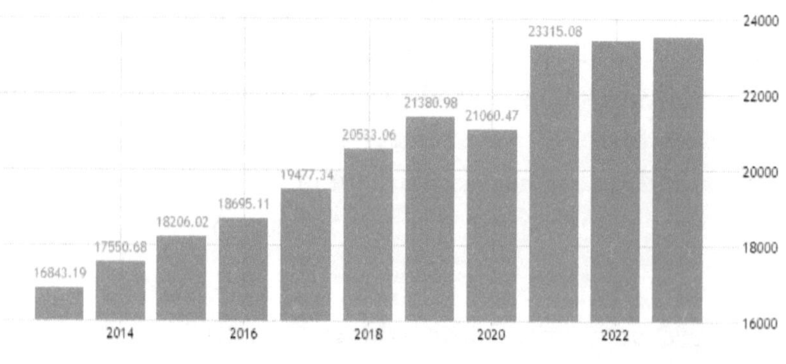

*Figure 11*

## Create your personal balance sheet or net worth statement

Creating a personal balance sheet or net worth statement is a powerful tool for understanding your financial situation. By taking stock of your assets and liabilities, you can clearly understand your net worth and make informed decisions about your financial future.

To create your balance sheet, list all. This might include cash and savings, investments, retirement accounts, real estate, and personal property. Be sure to include tangible assets, such as your home and car, and intangible assets, such as intellectual property or patents.

Next, list all your liabilities, such as mortgages, credit card debt, student loans, and other outstanding debts. Subtract your liabilities from your assets to determine your net worth. Ideally, your net worth should be positive, indicating that you have more assets than liabilities.

Once you have calculated your net worth, take a closer look at the numbers. Are you carrying a lot of debt? Are you putting enough money into savings or investments? Are there areas where you can reduce expenses or increase your income? Use your balance sheet as a starting point for making changes to your financial habits and setting new goals for the future.

It's also important to update your balance sheet regularly, at least once a year, to track your progress and make necessary adjustments. Over time, your net worth should grow as you pay down debt, increase your savings and investments, and accumulate more assets.

Creating a personal balance sheet is a simple yet powerful way to understand your current financial situation and take control of your financial future. Tracking your net worth over time allows you to set new goals, make informed decisions, and change your financial habits positively.

Before investing, you must evaluate your current financial standing and determine how much you must invest each month. Answer the following questions

1. Monthly income—after taxes and insurance, how much money gets deposited into your checking account?

2. List your monthly expenses: How much are you spending on average? Debt: What overhead do you have, and how much do you owe?

3. How much are you saving each month?

4. How much do you have saved as an emergency fund? This should be a minimum of 3 months.

You may decide how much money you can invest each month if you have a solid understanding of your monthly expenses. The objective is to be able to make monthly contributions to your investments so that they increase over time.

You may also want to make a personal balance sheet or net worth statement. Here's a description of it with an illustration.

After deciding what you want, you must create a schedule for achieving your objectives. The method you choose and the amount of risk you're willing to take will be influenced by your timeline. You have plenty of time to develop and bounce back from economic downturns, so you can afford to be more ambitious, for instance, if you want to earn money for retirement and retirement is 30 years away.

We frequently hear discussions on the advantages of fundamental vs. technical analysis in trading and investing. Both seek to raise our chances of making money. Therefore, both approaches can be effective when used correctly.

There is no argument between them because they are distinct from one another. Instead, it's a comparison of two entirely distinct strategies, and it's more of a "apples vs. oranges" kind of comparison.

## Rule of 72

The rule of 72 is a straightforward and practical calculator that may be used to determine when your investment will double. According to the formula, you may roughly estimate how many years it will take for your investment to double in value by dividing the number 72 by the annual rate of return on your investment. For instance, your investment will take around nine years to double if the yearly return is 8%. (72 divided by 8 equals 9). The rule of 72 is not precise, but it provides a quick and straightforward approach to analyze the potential development of your investments over time.

According to Albert Einstein, the eighth wonder of the world is compound interest. He earns it if he comprehends it. Whoever doesn't pays the price (Einstein, A).

Our daily lives depend heavily on math, which powers everything from the technologies we use to the cars we drive. While managing our funds and assets, math is crucial for determining values and achieving our financial objectives. The Rule of 72, which makes it simple to determine how long it will take for an investment to double in value based on its yearly rate of return, is one useful tool. Almost 500 years ago, this straightforward but effective method was originally recorded, and it is still a useful tool for investors today. We can reliably plan for the future and realize our financial goals by comprehending the Rule of 72. For instance, an investment with a 6% annual return can grow to an amazing $800,000 in 36 years, double in 12 years, and triple in 24 years. With math on our side, there is no end to the potential for financial success and progress.

By taking into account interest rates from credit card debt, auto loans, home mortgages, and school loans, the Rule of 72 can also be used to determine how many years it will take for someone else's money to double. For instance, the typical interest rate for credit cards is 17.3%. The result of 72 divided by that rate is 4.16 years.

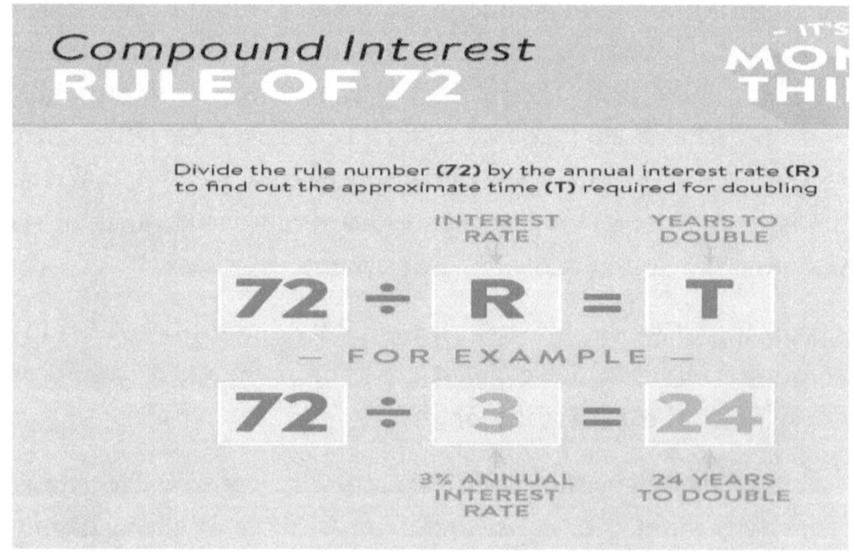


*Figure 12: Compound interest rule of 72*

## Find a Catalyst to propel your stocks.

The term "catalyst" describes anything that speeds up a rate of reaction or process. In chemistry, it describes a substance added to a reaction and increases the reaction rate.

In finance, a stock catalyst is an event, or expectation of an event, that drastically changes the price of a stock. For example, suppose a company releases an earnings report that is drastically different than what is expected. In that case, that could be a stock catalyst to change the security price drastically.

# CHAPTER 8: ECONOMIC INDICATORS FOR SMART INVESTING

## A BIG-PICTURE PERSPECTIVE

---

*"In the business world, the rearview mirror is always clearer than the windshield."* —**Warren Buffett**

---

Keeping track of the Federal Reserve's policies, government laws, and macroeconomic indicators is crucial because they together provide critical insights into the general health of the economy. Monitoring these variables allows companies, investors, and people to make more informed decisions about investments, financial planning, and consumption trends.

1. The Federal Reserve is in charge of implementing a stable monetary policy with the goal of promoting economic growth, controlling inflation, and regulating the supply of money in the economy. Inflation is one of the primary indicators that the

Fed monitors, with a target of roughly 3%. This rate indicates whether or not the economy's present price levels are increasing or dropping.

2. The unemployment rate is another critical measure. The Fed aims for an unemployment rate of 4.5% to 5%, which reflects the amount of people actively looking for work but are unable to find it. A greater unemployment rate suggests a weaker economy, whereas a lower unemployment rate indicates a more robust labor market.

3. Consumer confidence is another important measure to track since it represents consumers' general level of optimism about the economy. A satisfied customer is more inclined to spend money, which can fuel economic growth. The Fed normally targets a consumer confidence rate of 70% to 80%.

4. The Fed monitors interest rates in addition to inflation and unemployment rates. The goal is to keep interest rates stable and sustainable between 2% and 3%, which can encourage investment and expenditure while preventing inflation and economic instability.

5. Finally, the Federal Reserve's funds rate is an important signal. The fund's rate is the overnight interest rate at which banks lend money to one another. To guarantee that banks have ample liquidity to lend to consumers and companies, the Fed normally seeks a range of 2% to 5%.

Finally, tracking these five major economic variables provides insight into the overall health of the economy and aids in making wise financial and investment decisions. Following the Federal Reserve's policies and government laws is critical to establishing economic stability and long-term prosperity.

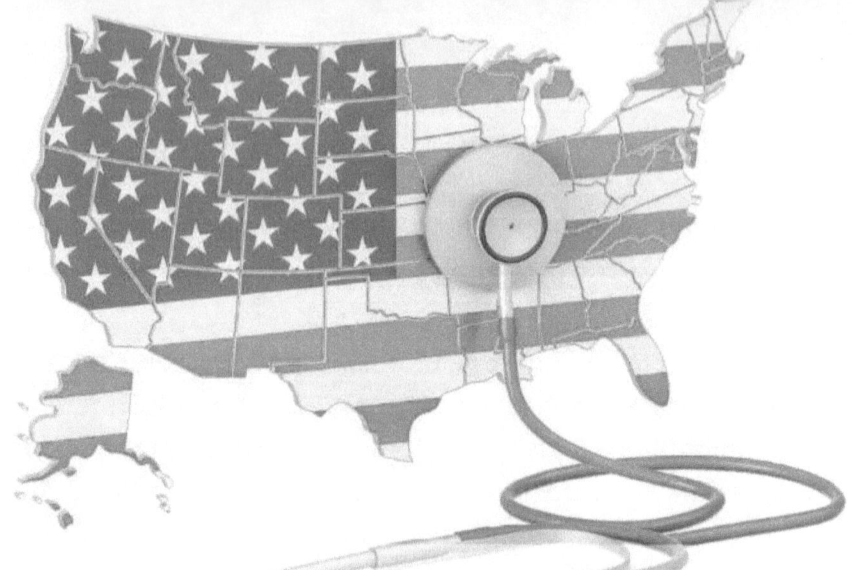

# CHAPTER 9: MONETARY VS. FISCAL POLICY

## A MICRO FRAMEWORK
## FOR FINANCIAL DECISIONS

"The art of taxation consists in so plucking the goose as
to obtain the largest possible amount of feathers with
the smallest possible amount of hissing."
—**Jean-Baptiste Colbert**

There was a young and ambitious entrepreneur named Alex. Alex had a great business idea and had secured some seed funding to start. However, as Alex started to delve deeper into the world of business and to invest, he realized that there was much he didn't understand, particularly regarding the macro-economy.

Feeling overwhelmed, Alex decided to take some time to educate himself. He read about monetary policy, which is how central banks influence the economy by managing the supply of money and credit. He learned about interest rates and inflation and how changes in these factors could impact his business.

He also read about fiscal policy, which is how governments use taxation and spending to influence the economy. Alex learned about the different types of government spending, such as infrastructure investment, and how they could create jobs and stimulate economic growth.

With this newfound knowledge, Alex could make better business and investing decisions. He could anticipate changes in interest rates and adjust his financing accordingly. He was also able to take advantage of government initiatives that supported small businesses like his own.

For example, when the government announced a tax credit for businesses that invested in renewable energy, Alex could quickly pivot and substantially invest in solar panels for his manufacturing facility. This helped him reduce his environmental impact and saved him money in the long run by lowering his energy bills.

As a result of his improved understanding of the macroeconomy, Alex's business thrived. He expanded his operations and created more jobs, which helped stimulate the local economy. He even mentored other young entrepreneurs, sharing his knowledge and helping them make better business decisions.

In the end, Alex's success showed that understanding monetary and fiscal policy is crucial for anyone who wants to succeed in business and invest. By staying informed and making intelligent decisions, it's possible to grow a successful business and contribute to society's greater good.

## Fiscal Policy Compared to Monetary Policy

Fiscal policy and monetary policy are two important tools governments, and central banks use to manage economic conditions and achieve policy goals.

Fiscal policy refers to the government's use of taxation and public spending to influence the economy. In other words, it involves the government's decisions about how much money it spends and how it collects that money through taxes. Fiscal policy can be used to stimulate economic growth, stabilize the economy during times of recession, and control inflation.

For example, during a recession, the government may increase its spending on infrastructure projects, creating jobs and boosting demand for goods and services. Similarly, during periods of high inflation, the government may raise taxes and reduce spending to reduce demand and inflationary pressures.

Monetary policy, on the other hand, refers to the actions taken by central banks to influence the money supply and interest rates in the economy. Monetary policy aims to maintain price stability and promote economic growth. Central banks can use a variety of tools to achieve these goals, such as adjusting the reserve requirements for banks, setting interest rates, and buying or selling government securities in the open market.

For example, suppose the central bank wants to stimulate economic growth. In that case, it may lower interest rates, which can make it cheaper for individuals and businesses to borrow money and invest in new projects. Similarly, if the central bank wants to combat inflation, it may raise interest rates to reduce the amount of money in circulation and slow down demand for goods and services.

Fiscal policy is concerned with government spending and taxation, while monetary policy is focused on the actions of central banks to influence the money supply and interest rates in the economy. Both policies are important tools for managing the economy and achieving policy goals, and they are often used in combination to achieve desired outcomes.

Monetary and fiscal policies are the two main levers a country can use to influence the economy (Forbes). Although they may sound similar because they both employ phrases that refer to money or finance, they are really different and are carried out by different departments of the government. The Federal Reserve is in charge of monetary policy, whereas the executive and legislative branches of the US government are in charge of fiscal policy.

In summary, Fiscal policy deals with taxation and public spending, according to Dr. Guy Baker, CFP, Ph.D., creator of Wealth Teams Alliance in Irvine, California. On the other hand, monetary policy aims to effect change by modifying the money supply (Forbes).

## The Effect of the Monetary Policies.

In the United States, central banks utilize monetary policy to control the amount of money in an economy. A central bank uses monetary policy to alter the supply of money and credit in the economy in an ongoing effort to keep employment, growth, and inflation on track.

According to Forbes, the Fed's "dual mandate" from Congress, which it pursues with monetary policy, is to increase employment and keep prices stable. That means the Fed wants to maintain a low unemployment rate rather than a zero rate in order to boost productivity without driving up inflation. Although there is no set target range, historically, the Fed has concentrated on maintaining an unemployment rate of between 3.5% and 4.5% (Forbes).

Regarding inflation, the Fed usually sets a target of 2% average annual price rises. Consumers and businesses are in a good position to spend, invest, and save enough cash reserves when unemployment is low, and inflation is hovering around the 2% level, which satisfies the Fed's mandate for a highly functional economy Forbes).

Robert Johnson, a professor of finance at Creighton University, asserts that the Fed's influence over these two important components of the economy is what gives it most of its power. The Fed uses its ability to regulate the money supply to carry out these objectives. It was given these duties in 1977 as a result of a joint Congressional directive, and it has a limited number of tools at its disposal to carry them out.

## Tools Used for Monetary Policy

The Federal Open Market Committee (FOMC) sets the fed funds rate, often known as the fed funds target rate, at its eight yearly meetings. When commercial banks overnight lend each other their excess reserves, they consider the fed funds rate (Forbes).

1.  Open market activities. In the open market, the Fed buys and sells government securities, including Treasury bonds and bills (Forbes). The Fed essentially raises the amount of money in circulation by repurchasing assets; on the other hand, lowering the supply by selling securities. Open market operations have traditionally been the most popular method

of implementing monetary policy.

2.  Requirements for reserves. Reserve requirements or the amount of cash banks must always maintain on hand to comply with banking regulations, are regularly watched by the Fed. In order to guarantee that they have money on hand in case consumers need it, those reserves must be safeguarded in bank safes or through deposits in accredited Federal Reserve Banks. The Fed can encourage banks to lend more money by reducing the amount of cash they must maintain on hand. It can also accomplish the opposite by increasing that demand.

3.  The Fed determines the discount or interest rate for short-term loans to financial institutions (Forbes). Typically, banks use these loans to fill reserve requirements or address liquidity issues that they are unable to solve through loans from other banks, which offer lower borrowing rates for federal funds. Discount rates are frequently high while the U.S. economy is booming because the Fed doesn't need to make borrowing money cheaply to stimulate activity. Yet, the Fed routinely lowers interest rates during economic downturns to promote lending and credit to both individuals and companies.

4.  According to Forbes, in quantitative easing (QE), a central bank like the Federal Reserve uses its enormous cash reserves to purchase big financial assets like stocks and bonds issued by governments and corporations. That might sound like open markets, but quantitative easing frequently involves purchasing longer-term government bonds as well. It also typically takes place when interest rates are already at or close to 0%, indicating that the Fed has already completely utilized one of its main weapons. Central banks must exercise caution

while using QE, though, as continuing to buy many assets could result in economic situations that monetary officials don't desire, such as increased inflation and asset bubbles (Forbes).

5. Messages of public service. A central bank will inform the financial markets and the broader public of its broad economic forecast and any policy actions it is taking when implementing a country's monetary policy. These PSAs alone may have the desired effects on the market and economy for the central bank.

## Key terms

- Hawks are policymakers who wish for higher interest rates to keep inflation in check.

- Inflation can arise when economic growth "overheats," and higher interest rates are viewed as reasonable by policymakers and advisors who advocate higher interest rates to control inflation.

- A dove, who favors a more accommodating interest rate policy to encourage economic spending, is the opposite of a hawk.

- Policymakers may adopt a hawkish or dovish attitude depending on the status of the American economy.

# CHAPTER 10: GOLD, SILVER, AND BEYOND

## INVESTING IN PRECIOUS METALS FOR PORTFOLIO GROWTH

"Gold is a treasure, and he who possesses it does all he wishes to in this world." —**Christopher Columbus**

As the world's economies began to reel under the pressure of hyperinflation shortly after COV ID, Bill knew he had to act fast. He had always been a savvy investor, but the current situation demanded more than just intelligent investments - it required a hedge against the relentless inflation threatening to cripple even the most robust economies.

Bill had always been intrigued by precious metals, particularly gold and silver. He knew these metals had been used throughout history as a store of value, a currency, and a hedge against inflation. But it was not until now, in the face of such an unprecedented crisis, that he realized how essential they could be to his investment portfolio.

He began to research the subject extensively, reading every book and article he could find. He learned about the various forms of gold and silver investments, from physical bullion to exchange-traded funds (ETFs), and the pros and cons of each. Bill soon became convinced that physical bullion was the best option for him. He began to scour the internet for reputable dealers and even visited a few in person to inspect their merchandise. He spent countless hours researching and reading about gold and silver coins and bars, their purity, and their historical significance.

As he began to amass his collection, Bill felt a sense of security that he had never experienced before. He knew that no matter how much inflation soared, his investment in precious metals would remain safe and secure. He was no longer at the mercy of the government or the central bank. He was in control of his financial future.

As he sat in his study, surrounded by his growing collection of gold and silver, Bill felt a sense of pride and accomplishment. He had made the right decision and knew his investment would serve him well for years. Years later, as he watched the financial world spin out of control, Bill knew that his decision to invest in precious metals had been the best he had ever made. He had secured his financial future and his family's and did it all on his terms.

Once, Tom Clancy said: "The elite always attempts to control knowledge, especially under a totalitarian type of government. Knowledge and information are powerful." (Clancy, T).  Bill had control over his financial future thanks to his expertise of investing in gold and silver, and he was confident that he would always be in charge.

## The End of an Era: Nixon's Shocking Announcement on the Gold Standard

Over five decades ago, President Nixon stunned the nation by declaring that the U.S. dollar would no longer be backed by gold, marking the end of the Bretton Woods system and an era of fixed gold prices. For almost 30 years, from 1944 to 1971, world currencies were pegged to the U.S. dollar, which was set at $35 per ounce of gold. However, this system was no longer sustainable, as governments were printing more money while still attempting to protect their gold reserves, causing the U.S. to have less than half of its gold reserves by the time of Nixon's announcement.

The era of fiat money had begun, leading to inflation and a sharp rise in the price of gold, which has long been a favorite safe-haven asset for investors during times of inflation. Fiat money is a type of currency that is not backed by a physical commodity, such as gold or silver, but instead derives its value from the government or other authority that issues it. The term "fiat" comes from the Latin word for "let it be done," which is an indication that the value of the money is determined by decree or mandate, rather than by intrinsic worth.

## The Appeal of Gold as Inflation Hedge in Current Times

Today, the U.S. is experiencing the highest inflation rates since that period, but it is due to supply and demand factors rather than dollar devaluation. As a result, gold is poised to continue its bullish run, and the question on many investors' minds is when this will happen. With its historical performance as a hedge against inflation, gold remains an attractive investment for those looking to protect their wealth.

The 1970s was a decade of high inflation and vital commodities that left a lasting impact on the market. During this period, the Consumer Price Index nearly doubled, causing the famous "Nifty Fifty" high-growth blue-chip companies to lose their edge due to unsustainable high valuations. Large-cap stocks returned less than 80% with dividends, and bonds outperformed stocks thanks to historically high-interest rates. However, the real star of the decade was gold, which soared after President Nixon abolished the gold standard, removing the limits on its price. By the end of the 1970s, the price of gold had risen more than 1,000%, beating all other major assets, as it lost the shackles of government limitations.

Gold's performance declined once the economy stabilized in the 1980s, setting a major low in 1999. However, since then, gold's price has increased more than six-fold, surpassing the total return of the stock market so far this century. Despite a strong dollar typically keeping gold from advancing too far, gold has outperformed the stock market by being viewed as a haven.

With its millennia-long history of reliably storing value, the yellow metal remains a great way to protect wealth against inflation and the possibility of another selloff. One convenient way to invest in gold is with SPDR Gold Shares (GLD), a popular exchange-traded fund that tracks precious metals' performance.

While gold's outperformance has faded over the past few months, the possibility of persisting inflation or a market fall could see gold shine again. Gold is an old-school, non-dividend-paying, unproductive asset that has consistently performed well in inflationary times.

Thus, it is a valuable investment option for those looking to protect their wealth and portfolio against the impacts of inflation.

## Silver's Promising Investment Future: The Growing Demand from Green Technologies

Over the years, many investors have chosen silver as their investment of choice because it is a precious metal. As the use of lithium batteries, solar panels, and electric cars has increased recently, so has the need for silver (EVs). Silver has a promising and appealing investment future as a result of these elements.

First and foremost, the rise of renewable energy has greatly increased the demand for lithium batteries. Lithium batteries have many uses, including in EVs, laptops, and cell phones. The International Energy Agency predicts that by 2030, 145 million electric vehicles will be on the road, up from 11 million in 2020. This will increase demand for lithium batteries, which will therefore raise silver demand.

Lithium-ion batteries, the most prevalent kind of battery used in EVs, are created using silver. The battery's cathode uses silver as a conductor, increasing the battery's endurance and efficiency. The demand for silver is anticipated to rise along with the demand for EVs.

Second, as the need for renewable energy has grown, so has the need for solar panels. The cost and efficiency of solar panels are rising, making them a desirable choice for homes and businesses. As more nations turn to renewable energy, it is anticipated that the use of solar panels would rise.

Due of its excellent conductivity and reflectivity, silver is a key component of solar panel manufacturing. The electrical connectors that assist in transferring the electricity produced by the solar panels to the grid are made of silver. The demand for silver is anticipated to rise along with the demand for solar panels.

The necessity to minimize carbon emissions has also increased the market for EVs. Governments all across the world are establishing regulations and rewards to encourage the use of EVs. In the upcoming years, this is anticipated to fuel the market for EVs.

Because of its excellent conductivity and longevity, silver is used in the manufacture of EVs. The electrical connectors and circuitry of EVs are made from silver. The demand for silver is anticipated to rise along with the demand for EVs.

It is anticipated that there will be a major growth in the demand for lithium batteries, solar panels, and EVs in the upcoming years. This will increase demand for silver, which is needed to make these goods. Investors seeking to profit from the rising demand for renewable energy will find silver to be a fascinating investment due to its good and promising future. In order to benefit from the potential rise in the silver market, investors should think about including silver in their investment portfolios.

## Gold and Silver Investing

Investing in gold and silver has long been considered a wise move for those looking to hedge against inflation. These precious metals have a unique ability to hold their value over time and provide a stability that can be invaluable in an uncertain economic climate. The chart below from goldprice.org displays the rise in Gold prices in USD from 1973 through April 2023.

*Figure 13: Gold prices since 1973*

Here are some reasons why gold and silver belong in every portfolio as a hedge against inflation:

**Inflation hedge**: Gold and silver have been historically used as an inflation hedge, meaning they retain their value over time as inflation rises. This is because the value of gold and silver is not tied to any specific currency or economy, making them a valuable tool to protect against the erosion of purchasing power that inflation can cause.

**Store of value:** Gold and silver have been a store of value for thousands of years, and they continue to hold their value today. Unlike paper currency, which can be easily manipulated and devalued by governments and central banks, gold and silver are tangible assets that can hold their value even during economic uncertainty.

**Diversification:** Including gold and silver in a diversified portfolio can help reduce risk and increase returns over the long term. This is because precious metals tend to move in the opposite direction of other asset classes, such as stocks and bonds, during economic turmoil.

**Limited supply:** The supply of gold and silver is limited; extracting these metals from the earth can be difficult and expensive. This means that the supply of gold and silver is unlikely to increase significantly over time, making them a valuable and scarce resource.

Over time, gold and silver have performed well as a hedge against inflation. Gold and silver prices rise as inflation increases, making them a valuable tool for protecting wealth. For example, during the inflationary period of the 1970s, the price of gold increased nearly 24 times its original value, while silver increased over 35 times. In recent years, gold and silver prices have continued to rise, with gold reaching record highs in 2020.

In conclusion, gold and silver investing can be a valuable addition to any portfolio, providing stability and protection against inflation. With a long history of holding their value and a limited supply, these precious metals offer unique benefits for investors looking to diversify and protect their wealth over time.

## How to invest in Gold and Silver

When purchasing gold and silver, several options are available to investors. Bullion coins or bars are the most popular investment in these precious metals. These items are produced by government mints or private companies and can be purchased through various dealers. Bullion coins and bars are a great choice for investors who want to hold physical metal and are looking for a long-term investment.

Another way to invest in gold and silver is through exchange-traded funds (ETFs). These funds hold physical metal and allow investors to buy and sell shares on the stock exchange. ETFs are a great choice for investors who want exposure to gold and silver but don't want to deal with the hassle of storing the physical metal.

Finally, investors can also invest in gold and silver through mining stocks. These stocks expose the mining industry and are a great way to invest in gold and silver without holding the physical metal. However, investing in mining stocks can be more volatile than investing in physical metal, as these stocks are subject to market forces and company-specific risks.

These precious metals have intrinsic value and can be easily bought and sold globally. Investors have various options when purchasing gold and silver, including bullion coins, ETFs, and mining stocks. By following these tips, investors can make a compelling and positive investment in gold and silver.

# CHAPTER 11: REAL ESTATE RICHES

## THE ALL-TIME BEST-PERFORMING ASSET CLASS

"Real estate cannot be lost or stolen, nor can it be carried away. Purchased with common sense, paid for in full, and managed with reasonable care, it is about the safest investment in the world."
—*Franklin D. Roosevelt*

Matt had always been a risk-taker as a real estate investor, but his latest venture had him on edge. He had sunk everything into a rundown apartment complex in the city's heart, and he knew it would take all his cunning to turn a profit. But Matt was a man who thrived on challenges. He meticulously planned his strategy, poring over every detail of the property's finances and researching the area's rental market. He was determined to make this investment work. Matt encountered obstacles at every turn as he set his plan into motion. The tenants were unruly; the building was in disrepair, and his competition was fierce. But Matt never lost sight of his goal. He worked tirelessly, negotiating with contractors, hiring a top-notch property management team, and keeping his finger on the market's pulse.

As weeks turned into months, Matt's hard work began to pay off. His once-shabby property began to shine with new paint, landscaping, and updated amenities. The tenants were happier and started spreading the word about the great place to live in town. Before long, Matt's property was the hottest ticket in town. He raised the rents, and they kept coming. His once-shaky investment had transformed into a cash cow. He had done it. He had succeeded.

With a satisfied smile, Matt took a moment to reflect on his journey. It had been a wild ride, full of ups and downs, but he had emerged victorious. He knew that this was just the beginning of his success in the world of real estate. He was already eyeing his next big project, and he knew that with his determination and skill, he could conquer anything that came his way.

Ultimately, Matt knew his hard work and determination had made all the difference. As he drove away from his property, he couldn't help but feel a sense of pride and accomplishment. He was a real estate investor who was damn good at it.

Real estate has been the go-to wealth builder for millionaires for centuries because it follows the money. When inflation rises, so do home values. When inflation cools, home prices will drop but the overall home value changes by little.

It also lets you take advantage of leverage. Leverage is the use of borrowed money or debt to increase the possible return on an investment. Most of the time, you use cash or a mortgage to get a loan for your real estate investment. Leverage is good if the value of your real estate goes up, but it can be expensive if prices go down. Leverage is a way to use borrowed money to get a higher return on an investment. If the return on the whole amount invested in the security (your cash plus the money you borrowed) is more than the interest you pay on the borrowed money, you can make a big profit.

The majority of the time, a 20% down payment (together with a solid credit history) entitles you to 100% of the land and home you desire. 20% down indicates you're using 80% of your available credit; some mortgage programs can even allow you to put down less.

## Become a Landlord and Earn Rental Income

As someone who has been a landlord, I can tell you firsthand that investing in real estate is no walk in the park. It requires hard work, dedication, and effort. However, the benefits can be extraordinary if you put in the time and energy.

First and foremost, real estate investing can provide you with a steady stream of monthly cash flow that increases with inflation. Rental property ownership is a way to earn passive income from tenants (Dilendorf, 2021). Additionally, owning rental properties can lead to generous tax deductions such as mortgage interest, depreciation, repair and maintenance costs, travel expenses, home office expenses, and insurance costs. These deductions can significantly reduce your tax burden and increase your profits.

Another benefit of real estate investing is that renters pay off your mortgage and increase your equity in the property. This can help you build wealth over time and provide additional income streams.

Real estate investing also offers financial leverage through OPM (Other People's Money), which can dramatically increase your returns on every dollar invested. Furthermore, capital appreciation of the property's value can increase your net worth, making it a powerful wealth-building tool.

Investing in real estate is also an excellent way to diversify your portfolio, especially if you are overweighed in paper assets. By owning rental properties, you can create a balanced portfolio that includes tangible and intangible assets (real estate) (stocks, bonds, etc.).

To be successful in real estate investing, there are a few simple suggestions that I have found to be useful. First, it is important to stay liquid by maintaining a six-month emergency fund. This will allow you to take advantage of investment opportunities as they arise.

Location is also crucial. Stick to areas with growing populations, desirable school districts, low unemployment rates, and nearby shopping centers. If a local college or university is nearby, consider that a plus.

Selecting three-bedroom, two-bathroom homes or larger ones is essential when choosing properties. Avoid two-bedroom homes, as they tend to have a higher turnover rate. Additionally, three-bedroom homes typically sell much faster than two-bedroom homes.

When financing your properties, only consider fixed-rate mortgages. Adjustable-rate mortgages may have low upfront interest rates but can lead to financial distress when interest rates rise.

Finally, consider hiring a property management company to handle day-to-day operations. They can take care of most of the headaches in exchange for a portion of your monthly profits. This will allow you to focus on higher-income activities, such as finding more properties or developing additional income streams.

Real estate investing is a challenging but rewarding way to build wealth and create financial security. With careful planning, sound financial management, and hard work, you can reap the benefits of real estate investing and achieve your financial goals.

## Is rental property ownership right for you?

Ask yourself the following questions to find out if it would be a good idea for you to rent a home. If you answered "yes" to any of these questions, renting out a property could be a great way to start making extra money.

## 1. Do I own the house I live in?

Robert Kiyosaki, who wrote Rich Dad, Poor Dad, has always said that your home is not an investment; it's just a place to live. You can, however, turn your home into an investment. "Since I started working in real estate, many of the homes I've lived in have had a "lock off" or an apartment attached, built-in, or added on so that renters could help pay part of my mortgage. I use this method to help keep the costs low to buy more real estate. Make sure you own your home first, and then turn it into an asset to start bringing in money.

## 2. Do you have enough cash for 3–6 months?

Real estate can be a hard-to-sell asset, and you don't want to be forced to sell when the market is down because you don't have any savings.

## 3. Do I have an account for repairs and vacancies?

You need "holding power," which means that your investments should be able to handle stress. Too many investors lose a lot of money because they don't plan for a house to be empty for a few months or for a bad renter to trash it. Make sure this doesn't happen to you. Plan for the worst, but hope for the best!

## 4. Is real estate and what it has to offer interesting to you?

Do you want to search for house opportunities? Do you want to be able to own a house or building whose mortgage is paid by tenants? If that's what you want, rental property is a great place to look.

## How does rental real estate work?

Using rental real estate for cash flow is not as complicated as it seems. The key to making it work and getting a steady cash flow is to find a quality property with a meager vacancy rate. In other words, you must do your homework. Putting in time and effort before you make your purchase can be advantageous for years.

The way you should approach rental real estate is from a long-term perspective. The goal of buying a rental property is to rent it out for more than your holding costs (mortgage, insurance, property tax and maintenance) so that you earn a profit each month. For example, buying a home that costs you $1,000 a month but can be rented out for $1,200 a month will mean you get a $200 profit each month. So, if you make a $200 profit after you pay all your expenses, and your initial down payment is $20,000, your cash-on-cash return is 12% ($200 X 12 for yearly cash flow, divided by down payment). That should get you excited enough to get started! Many properties can give you substantial returns.

"I aim for at least 8% and have had some closer to 15%." Very few places can make that kind of return in today's economic environment. In addition to the cash flow, your property can appreciate over time, but even if your property does not appreciate, you are still making a stream of income.

The key to growing your income with rental real estate is duplication. Over time, you find more and more opportunities to duplicate your success. For instance, buying and renting out one property is excellent. However, more properties successfully managed within your portfolio mean higher cash flow and overall net worth. Think about it. Would you rather have one property bringing in $200 in cash per month or ten properties with a cash flow of $2,000 or more monthly? Which scenario would you want, 20 years later when your tenants pay off all the mortgages? How great is it that you are getting a free house given to you by your renters over the given period?

## Why own rental real estate

Real estate investing has proven to be one of the most reliable and profitable asset classes. The wealthy have long known the power of real estate to create generational wealth and financial security.

Consider the story of Sarah, a young investor who started buying rental properties in her mid-twenties. Over the next decade, Sarah continued to acquire properties, using the rental income to pay down mortgages and reinvesting in more real estate. Today, in her late thirties, Sarah owns a substantial real estate portfolio that generates significant passive income, allowing her to live on her terms.

This success story is not unique. Real estate investing has been a proven wealth-building strategy for centuries, offering steady returns and a hedge against inflation. Whether buying and holding rental properties, flipping homes, or investing in commercial properties, there are many ways to profit from real estate.

Moreover, real estate has several advantages over other asset classes. Unlike stocks which can be volatile and unpredictable, real estate offers a tangible, physical asset that can be improved and maintained over time. Additionally, real estate investors can take advantage of tax benefits, such as depreciation and mortgage interest deductions.

Real estate investment remains one of the all-time best-performing assets, and for a good reason. The wealthy have long known the power of real estate to create long-term wealth, and everyday investors can benefit as well. Real estate investing can help investors achieve financial freedom and build a legacy for future generations by taking a long-term approach and focusing on cash flow. Rental property is a basic income stream.

Real estate has made many commoners rich—real wealth—backed by a physical asset. Real estate ownership made 90% of millionaires, according to Andrew Carnegie. The Bible mentions land ownership many times. "Look, I have placed the nation before you; go in and possess the land," The Bible mentions "soil" over 1,700 times, suggesting God cherishes it. "Land" is now called "real estate." God made real estate a great investment.

Furthermore, rental real estate can provide some inflation protection for your investment, as rents typically increase over time. Rents are very likely to continue increasing due to numerous economic trends that are leading Americans to rent instead of own. Many economic reasons can raise housing rents. These trends include:

1.  Housing availability and demand affect rent prices first. Due to little supply and great demand, landlords can charge more for rent. Rents might also rise if population growth outpaces construction.

2.  Second, inflation affects housing rents. Inflation raises the cost of building materials, labor, and other inputs, which raises the rent. Inflation can also devalue rental income, prompting landlords to raise rates.

3.  Thirdly, interest rates affect home rents. Low-interest rates can encourage homebuyers to take out loans, reducing the availability of rental properties and raising rents. High-interest rates can deter homebuyers and increase demand for rentals, which might raise rents.

4.  Property taxes and maintenance might raise rents. Landlords may have to raise rents to meet these costs and stay profitable.

## Future Growth in the Rental Market

Several demographic and economic trends are likely to drive the rental market's growth in the coming years.

First of all, more and more millennials and Gen Z, who are now the biggest and most diverse generations in history, are choosing to rent instead of buying a home. This is because of a number of things, such as high student debt, high housing costs, and a desire for more freedom in how they live.

Second, the aging of the baby boomer generation is also likely to help the rental market grow. Many people who are retiring and downsizing are selling their homes instead of buying another one. This trend is especially clear in cities, where many baby boomers want to move into smaller homes to enjoy city life's ease and convenience.

Third, the rise of the gig economy and working from home will also likely help the rental market grow. As more people work from home and have more freedom in their jobs, they may be more likely to rent and be able to move for work or personal reasons more often.

Last but not least, immigration and population growth in cities are likely to also help the rental market grow. As more people move to cities, the housing demand is likely to increase. This could cause rents to increase and more people to invest in rental properties.

In short, demographic and economic trends like people waiting longer to buy homes, baby boomers downsizing, the gig economy, remote work, and population growth in cities are likely to drive the future growth market for renters.

According to the Urban Institute's Housing Commission report, the number of renters is expected to grow by over 5 million by 2022. More than 35% of households in the U.S. rent homes, according to 2017-2021 data from the U.S. Census Bureau.

Rising unemployment and tightened loan qualification standards have turned many would-be homebuyers into renters. Rents are creeping up in many areas of the country due to the rising demand for rental homes. Food and shelter are two basic needs that will never change for people, and rental real estate provides a great way to supply those needs and create a sizeable, steady income.

As the pandemic made working from home more popular, renters with a lot of money started looking for bigger homes in areas that used to be cheaper. This migration increased rents in the suburbs more than it decreased them in the city, so rents went up overall.

Expert investors will tell you that 2009, or 14 years ago, was the best time to invest in rental property. Inflation has caused interest rates to go up a lot in recent months, but they are still pretty low.

## Rental Real Estate Income

Look no further than real estate investing for cash flow. Real estate investing is a lucrative way to earn passive income (Geske, 2011). While generating significant cash flow with an active income stream can be challenging, investing in rental properties can be both enjoyable and rewarding. With returns ranging from 5 to 25% and beyond, real estate offers a reliable source of passive income that can help you achieve your financial goals while allowing you to focus on the things that truly matter to you. And the best part? You'll build a portfolio of assets that will continue to appreciate over time, providing long-term security and stability for you and your loved ones. So why wait? Start exploring the possibilities of rental property income today and experience the benefits of financial freedom and peace of mind

In order to generate income, an income property is acquired and improved. Residential properties that generate income include single-family homes, multi-family residences, and commercial buildings. Owners earn by keeping the property in their possession and renting it out while its value increases before selling it for a profit.

# Tax Rental Real Estate and write off

Investors aim to gain from rental property ownership in addition to the long-term income generation and owner equity growth. Comparing investing in rental property to other income-producing assets, there are many tax advantages.

Beginner real estate investors are frequently pleasantly pleased to discover how accommodating the American tax system is to them. The greatest tax advantages of owning rental property are summarized in the following points.

1.  Deducting operating and owner expenditures, depreciation, deferring capital gains taxes, and avoiding FICA tax are the key tax advantages of owning rental property.

2.  The majority of the time, a rental property's income is taxed according to the investor's federal income tax bracket as ordinary income.

3.  When a shareholder engages in a 1031 tax-deferred exchange, capital gains tax and depreciation recapture tax may be postponed.

4.  According to the IRS, real estate investors must maintain accurate records and a paper trail to be eligible for the tax advantages of owning a rental property.

Your most significant tax break is the ability to deduct your property's purchase price through a predetermined schedule of depreciation, even if the property is appreciating. Additionally, there are other deductions that you can take advantage of, including deducting mortgage interest, borrowing against your equity, and depreciating your property for up to 27.5 years. You can also deduct interest on credit cards used for property purchases, insurance, maintenance repairs, travel expenses, legal and professional fees, and property taxes. You can also avoid capital gains if you've lived on the property for the last two out of five years.

## Online Resources

Online resources for buying and selling houses are one of the easiest and most popular ways to search for and view houses. These resources allow buyers and sellers to connect without the need for a physical real estate agent. Here's a summary of how it works:

- Websites such as Zillow, Redfin, and Realtor.com provide a database of homes for sale.

- Buyers can filter their search based on their budget, location, number of bedrooms, and other features.

- Once a buyer finds a house they are interested in, they can reach out to the seller directly through the website or app.

The online resources of Redfin, Zillow, and Trulia and their house evaluation estimators are in competition with one another. Redfin may be the easiest to use. It has a simple interface that doesn't bombard you with information but offers almost everything you need to know about the house.

## 8 Steps to Get Started with Rental Real Estate

Using real estate as a cash source is all about following the steps that have been proven to work throughout many decades. If you follow the steps below, along with some education and research, you will set yourself up for success.

## 1. Begin with why and mission.

Why buy rental properties? What is your goal? Create your mission statement from these responses. Cynthia Goda, a real estate investor, says: I provide quality properties for quality tenants where they can call home and make lasting memories. I get a good lifetime income."

## 2. Get funding.

Get finance to start renting real estate. Several avenues exist for funding. Bank or mortgage company loans or cash purchases are the most popular methods. Home equity loans are another possibility. Goda bought a $56,000 home with a home equity line. The renter paid off the loan in a few years after renting it for $750. Goda owns the house outright and receives rent checks from the renter. Owner financing is another option.

## 3. Locate a great agent

Agents are your best allies. A good real estate agent can help you find houses and evaluate local property values and rents. Join a local real estate investment group. These groups meet regularly and discuss financial themes in every major city. Other investors, funding sources, and property sellers will also be present. Watch real estate shows, read books by real estate moguls, attend to open houses, ask plenty of questions, and study the real estate profession. Knowledge breeds success.

## 4. Know state law.

Despite its illogic, you cannot do whatever you want with your property. Federal, state, and municipal governments regulate rental property use. You cannot visit the property "just because" even though it is yours. Security deposits cannot be collected at will. Almost half of U.S. states limit rent collection to one or two months. When investing in rental property, consider these areas:

State-specific Landlord-Tenant Legislation. You can locate these on your state government's website.

- FCRA. Landlords must provide applicants with a "adverse action notice" if they deny a lease based on consumer report information. Check out the FTC's website.

- FHA. This law forbids leasing discrimination based on race, color, religion, sex, national origin, familial status, and handicap.

- Lead Disclosure. Before renting a pre-1978 home or apartment, you must warn tenants about lead-based paint. Otherwise, you might be fined $11,000. See www.epa.gov.

- Section 8. You must read the rules before joining this low-income housing program.

- Local regulations. Local laws may supplement state and federal laws. Be compliant!

- Labor laws. If you employ someone. Regulations abound.

- Service animals. If a resident has a physician-documented assistance animal, landlords cannot impose pet deposits or monthly fees.

- Eviction rules. If you need to evict a renter, careful research can help. Little mistakes might cost you.

- Security Deposit Rules. Know what you can charge in your state.

## 5. Locate Your Property

Maintain your criteria. You may want single-family homes, multi-family homes, or apartments. Finding a property that meets your investing goals is the next stage to making money from a rental property.

## 6. Optional: Form a rental LLC.

A Limited Liability Corporation (LLC) protects you from renters who may sue you and the property. Just get a lawyer. It's expensive but worth it. Owning each home in a different LLC is also smart. Discuss your rental real estate business structure with an attorney. Liability insurance, or "umbrella coverage," extends beyond homeowner's insurance.

## 7. Enhance the property

Fixing up a cheap property will make it more appealing. If so, make those tiny noticeable improvements now. Remember that consumers pay for substance, therefore, anything they can see will be more satisfying than something they can't (think light fixtures, countertops, and paint accents). These inexpensive upgrades boost rent and cash flow.

## 8. Hire a property manager

Decide if you'll handle or outsource your rental properties. Both have merit. You can increase your profit margin by renting homes yourself. Use a property management company if you don't have time or desire anonymity. These firms charge 8–10% of gross monthly rent. For this fee, they will market, screen, pick renters, collect rent, manage property upkeep and repairs, and other services depending on your chosen firm. As the management company approaches every property as a business, the tenant won't take advantage of you. Property managers issue monthly checks, making them fun to use!

**"Rental troubles" are one reason people leave the rental real estate business. Ask yourself, "How can I avoid the same problem?"**

## You can be a landlord

As I write this, in mid-2023, housing prices dropped after the considerable price rise during the pandemic. Many people were moving out of the congested big cities to more economical houses where they could own more and work remotely.

Many years ago, after having one of my first rental properties, I was excited to get the house rented and about being a landlord. I ended up with a huge learning experience as I had the worst tenants ever. The family of five left the house with a couple of thousands of dollars in repairs to be made and owning me three months of rent. I learned how important tenant selection is.

The best way to secure long-term tenants is to advertise on Facebook marketplace, newspaper or use Craigslist or other popular websites. State in your ad that you are looking for long-term renters. This doesn't necessarily mean signing a long-term lease (a different topic altogether) is always best, but you want long-term renters. After receiving applications from prospective renters, ALWAYS do the following steps:

1.  Perform a background check. The reason here is apparent.

You do not want known criminals in your rental property.

2. Request a consumer report. One great way to use these reports is to verify information in the application. Make sure your selection criteria are the same for everyone. Be sure to follow the guidelines of your state and the Fair Credit Reporting Act.

3. Call all references and previous landlords. Be cautious, though, because the previous landlord could tell you what you want to hear to get a bad tenant out of their property. Therefore, performing all three steps listed here besides the application is essential.

Waiting for a good tenant is easier than evicting a bad one. Here is a Verification Tip (courtesy of The Landlord Survival Guide, by Jeffrey Taylor) Applicants sometimes use friends as landlords or employers. Hence, by asking a question the reference must answer correctly, you can rapidly authenticate their authenticity. If an applicant says his rent is $750, inquire if he pays $850. If the caller answers yes, it's not the landlord. Hence, gently end the phone contact and proceed to the next reference. You may find the landlord or reject this applicant.

## Real Estate challenges

Persistent difficulties, also known as "rental headaches," are one of the leading causes of people leaving the rental real estate industry. For instance, a landlord might have a tenant who consistently pays rent after the due date or another tenant who phones every other week to report minor maintenance issues (like changing a light bulb). Many landlords lose their cool and decide to quit their jobs or choose a very boring lifestyle. Yet, if you and your team are ready for these difficulties, your likelihood of experiencing ongoing problems will be lower. First, start out with the attitude that you WILL face difficulties. Second, when difficulties arise, take precautions to ensure they won't happen again rather than just putting out the fire to narrowly avoid tragedy. "What can I do differently to prevent the same situation from occurring again?" is a good question to ask yourself. Consider fixing the issue yourself rather than immediately blaming your renter.

# CHAPTER 12: SIDE HUSTLES AND ENTREPRENEURSHIP

## BUILDING INCOME OUTSIDE OF 9-TO-5

> "The best way to predict the future is to create it."
> —**Peter Drucker**

### Side hustle businesses

As one of my prior students called, Monica walked through the campus; she couldn't help but feel a sense of restlessness. Her current job as a software engineer was stable, but it didn't ignite her passion. She wanted more out of life, and he knew she had the skills to start her own business. Monica had always been fascinated by the world of entrepreneurship and had spent countless hours reading books and attending seminars.

One day, Monica decided to take the leap and start her side hustle.

She envisioned an app that would revolutionize how people order food from restaurants. She spent every free moment working on his idea, pouring her heart and soul into the project. It wasn't easy; she had to learn new programming languages, refine her marketing strategy, and convince investors to believe in her vision. But she was determined to succeed.

As the weeks turned into months, Monica's entrepreneurship side hustle started to take shape. She spent long hours in coffee shops and co-working spaces, networking with other entrepreneurs and hustling to secure funding. Her friends and family thought he was crazy for taking such a risk, but Monica knew she was onto something big.

Finally, after what felt like an eternity of hard work, Monica's app was ready to launch. She threw a launch party in a trendy downtown venue, inviting investors, journalists, and foodies from all over the city. As she stood up to give his pitch, she felt a surge of excitement and adrenaline rush through his veins.

"Welcome, everyone, to the future of food ordering," she began, her voice ringing out with conviction. "My app will change how you think about ordering food. No more waiting in long lines; no more frustration with inaccurate orders. With our app, you can order your food with just a few clicks and deliver it straight to your doorstep."

The room erupted in applause and cheers. Monica knew that he had nailed her pitch, and she felt a sense of pride and accomplishment wash over her. From that moment on, her side hustle became her full-time job, and he never looked back.

Years later, she emailed me, letting me know I motivated her as a student in one of my classes. She expressed to me how far she had come. Her app had become a household name, and she had built a thriving business with a team of dedicated employees. She knew she had made the right decision to pursue her dream of entrepreneurship, and she felt grateful for the opportunity to live his life on his terms.

She thanked me again for motivating her; now, she knows the sky is the limit. Anything was possible with hard work, passion, and a little luck.

## Opportunities for entrepreneurs

Entrepreneurship can be an exciting and rewarding path for those willing to take risks and work hard. With the right idea, skills, and resources, anyone can turn their passions and problems into opportunities for success. However, it's important to understand what makes an idea a good opportunity before leaping.

A good opportunity meets customers' needs. It's important to identify a gap in the market and create a product or service that solves a problem for potential customers. This is the foundation of a successful business, satisfying customers' needs and desires.

The next step is to assess your skills and resources. Do you have what it takes to start and run a business? This includes having the necessary technical skills, financial resources, and management expertise to keep the business afloat. If you lack any of these, you must seek partners or advisors who can help fill the gaps.

It's also important to consider pricing and profitability. While offering a product or service at a reasonable price, ensuring the business is profitable is equally important. This means calculating the costs of production, marketing, and other expenses and setting a price that will allow you to make a profit.

Timing is another crucial factor to consider. You must get your product or service to customers before the window of opportunity closes. This means understanding the market, the competition, and other factors that could affect your success. With the right timing, your business can take off and grow rapidly.

There are many reasons why people choose to become entrepreneurs. For some, it's the opportunity to pursue their passion and create something they believe in. For others, it is a chance for profit and financial independence. Still, others are drawn to the challenge and excitement of starting and running a business.

Regardless of your motivation, entrepreneurship can be a fulfilling and rewarding journey. You can turn your ideas into a successful business by identifying a good opportunity, assessing your skills and resources, and understanding the market.

## What does it take to be an entrepreneur?

Being an entrepreneur is not just a job or career choice; it's a lifestyle. Entrepreneurs create and run businesses, taking on financial risks to achieve success. However, not everyone is cut out for this challenging role. It takes a certain type of person with specific qualities to succeed in this field.

Firstly, entrepreneurs need to be self-directed and self-nurturing. They have to be their boss, set their own goals, and motivate themselves to achieve them. Working independently is essential, as there is no one to hold them accountable for their actions but themselves.

Entrepreneurs also need to be highly action-oriented, as they are responsible for driving their business forward. They need to be proactive and take the initiative to make things happen. They must be willing to put in the effort required to make their dreams a reality.

In addition, entrepreneurs need to be highly energetic. Running a business can be physically and emotionally draining, and entrepreneurs need the stamina and drive to push through the tough times. They need to be able to work long hours and handle the stress and pressure that comes with being a business owner.

Finally, entrepreneurs must be tolerant of uncertainty. Starting a new business is inherently risky, and success is not guaranteed. Entrepreneurs must be comfortable with the unknown and willing to take calculated risks to achieve their goals.

Being an entrepreneur requires unique qualities, including self-direction, action orientation, high energy, and tolerance for uncertainty. Those who possess these traits are more likely to be successful in the challenging yet rewarding world of entrepreneurship

## The Gig economy

In recent years, the gig economy has exploded in popularity as more and more people turn to side hustles to supplement their income. According to Zapier.com, one in three Americans currently works a side hustle, and a staggering 24% of Americans plan to start a new gig or side hustle this year.

The rise of e-commerce has also played a significant role in the gig economy's growth. In 2020, online sales reached an impressive $813 billion, representing a 42% increase over the previous year.

Moreover, in 2019, e-commerce sales accounted for 11% of all retail sales in the United States. The Statista Digital Market Outlook projects that revenue will continue to grow, reaching an estimated $563.4 billion by 2025.

These figures indicate a growing trend towards entrepreneurship and self-employment, with many individuals seeking to create their own opportunities and income streams. A recent survey found that 45% of working Americans report having a side hustle, translating to roughly 70 million people. Among millennials, this statistic rises to a staggering 50%.

To succeed in the gig economy, individuals must possess certain qualities, including self-direction, action orientation, high energy levels, and a tolerance for uncertainty. With the right mindset and skill set, anyone can tap into the growing gig economy and build a successful side hustle or new business venture. Here are some of the gigs the become popular in the gig economy.

## Freelance Writing

In the modern world, there are many prospects for writers to establish a reliable source of income thanks to the enormous growth of the freelance writing sector. Freelance writing is a great way to earn income from the comfort of your own home (Romero, 2020). Writing for several customers and media on a freelance basis without being employed full-time is known as freelancing. Because of the rise of the internet and the desire for high-quality content, many authors now have access to a reliable source of income through freelance writing.

The flexibility offered by freelance writing is a huge benefit. As they can work from any location at any time, freelance writers can balance numerous sources of income. For instance, a freelancer can spend the morning writing a blog post for one client, the afternoon writing an article for a magazine, and the evening working on a book project. Hence, freelance writing can be done on the side while working a full-time job or managing another business.

The variety of jobs accessible is another benefit of using freelance writing as numerous income streams. A wide range of clients, including magazines, newspapers, websites, blogs, and other media, are available for freelance writers to work for. As a result, they can diversify their sources of income and lower the risk associated with doing so. Additionally, freelance writers can meet the demands of various clients by specializing in a variety of topics, like travel, technology, finance, and health.

Freelance writing can be financially rewarding depending on the sort of writing and the client's budget. While some customers pay by the word, others pay by the project. Additionally, independent writers are free to haggle over fees and raise prices for complex or urgent assignments. Furthermore, freelance writers can generate passive revenue by producing eBooks, developing courses, or marketing their work on websites like Amazon or Etsy.

In order to be successful as a freelance writer, you must possess excellent writing abilities, a steady internet connection, and a computer or laptop. Also, independent authors must effectively market their offerings and compile a body of work to serve as a portfolio of their abilities. They can also look for clients by participating in online writing communities or by using freelancing markets like Upwork, Fiverr, or Freelancer.

Freelancing can be an attractive multiple stream of income for authors who enjoy writing and have the required abilities and perseverance to succeed. Flexibility, a variety of opportunities, and the possibility for substantial income are all provided by freelancing. To succeed as a freelance writer, you must put in a lot of effort and be persistent.

## Affiliate Marketing

An affiliate in affiliate marketing receives a commission for advertising the goods or services of another business online. Affiliate marketing is a way to earn income by promoting products or services on your website or social media channels (Tran, 2021). It is disseminating information about the goods or services to a target audience using a special affiliate link that keeps track of referrals and purchases made through the link. With good reason, affiliate marketing has gained popularity as a method to create numerous streams of income.

The reduced overhead costs of affiliate marketing are a key benefit. Affiliate marketers are exempt from developing a good or service, dealing with customer support, or managing shipping and handling. The sole responsibility is to promote the goods or services to a target audience through different marketing platforms, including a blog, social media, or email marketing.

Earning passive income is another benefit of affiliate marketing. Once the affiliate has produced content to advertise the goods or services, the affiliate link may still bring in money even if the affiliate is not actively pushing it. As a result, affiliate marketing can be pursued as a side business in addition to full-time employment or other enterprises.

A great earning potential is also provided via affiliate marketing. Although affiliate product compensation rates might vary, some businesses provide commissions of up to 50% or more. When more people use the affiliate link to make referrals, the earning potential likewise grows. The possibility of receiving more commissions rises as the affiliate expands their following and gains the confidence of their followers.

The choice of a niche must be in line with the affiliate's interests and area of competence if they are to be successful as affiliate marketers. Also, the affiliate should pick goods or services with a high conversion rate that are pertinent to their target market. Gaining the audience's trust is essential, thus the affiliate should only advocate goods and services they firmly believe in and have personally tried.

For Gig workers wishing to supplement their income without expending a lot of time and effort, affiliate marketing can be a tempting additional stream of income. Low overhead expenses, the capacity to generate passive income, and a high earning potential are all features of affiliate marketing. But, choosing the appropriate niche, advertising goods or services that are in line with the interests of the audience, and gaining their confidence is necessary for affiliate marketing success

## Online teaching and tutoring

Due to the rising demand for online education, online teaching and tutoring have emerged as well-liked methods of creating numerous streams of income. Online teaching and tutoring can be a great way to earn income while helping others learn (Lee, 2020). Delivering instructional material to students using online platforms like Zoom,

Skype, or Google Meet is the basis of online teaching and tutoring.

The flexibility that online instruction and tutoring provide is one of its key benefits. With the flexibility to work from anywhere and at any time, online teachers and tutors may balance several income streams. An online instructor, for instance, might assist a student in the afternoon, teach a class in the morning, and create course materials in the evening. This means that, in addition to doing a full-time job or managing another business, one can employ online teaching and tutoring as a side business.

The variety of opportunities offered is another benefit of online instruction and tutoring. From elementary school through university level, online instructors and tutors can teach various disciplines and courses. They can also specialize in a variety of fields, such as academic tutoring, music instruction, or teaching foreign languages. As a result, they can diversify their sources of income and lower the risk associated with doing so.

Depending on the sort of instruction and the client's budget, online tutoring and teaching can be financially rewarding. While some customers pay by the hour, others pay by the project. Also, online instructors and tutors have the option to haggle over fees and raise prices for more complex assignments. Online course sales and educational content creation for online platforms are additional passive income opportunities for online teachers and tutors.

Strong teaching abilities, a steady internet connection, and a computer or laptop are requirements for success as an online tutor or teacher. Additionally, online instructors and tutors must effectively market their offerings and compile a portfolio of their teaching and tutoring accomplishments to demonstrate their qualifications.

In order to find students, they can also sign up with websites like Udemy, Coursera, or Chegg that offer tutoring services. Creating and selling online courses can be a profitable way to earn income from your expertise (Nesbit, 2020)

For those who enjoy tutoring and have the abilities and drive to achieve, online teaching and instructing can be a lucrative multiple stream of income. Flexibility, a variety of options, and the possibility for substantial income are all provided by online teaching and tutoring. Yet, developing a fruitful career as an online teacher or tutor takes effort, commitment, and perseverance.

## E-Commerce

E-commerce, or online sales, has gained popularity as a way to create various income streams. E-commerce involves selling products online through an online store or marketplace (Rabie, 2020). Selling goods or services online through a website or an online marketplace like Amazon or eBay is known as e-commerce. E-commerce is a desirable alternative for anyone trying to make extra money since it has a number of benefits.

The capacity to reach a larger audience is a significant benefit of e-commerce. By connecting with clients worldwide through an online store or marketplace, retailers can increase their chances of making sales. E-commerce is also convenient for both buyers and sellers. Customers may purchase from the comfort of their homes, while sellers can run their businesses anywhere and anytime.

The minimal overhead costs of e-commerce are another benefit. E-commerce companies don't need a physical location or to pay rent, unlike conventional brick-and-mortar stores. The only expenditures involved are those for the product or service, website hosting, and upkeep. This makes e-commerce a viable choice for people wishing to launch a business or supplement their income.

E-commerce has a significant revenue potential as well. The possibility for sales rises with the size of the audience, and sellers are free to establish their prices and profit margins. E-commerce companies can also generate passive money through sponsored postings, affiliate marketing, and product reviews.

It's critical to pick the best goods or services to sell and market them skillfully if you want to succeed in e-commerce. In order to reach their target audience, sellers should undertake market research to determine the goods or services that are in demand. They should then employ online marketing tactics like SEO, social media marketing, and email marketing. In order to earn customers' trust, vendors should also deliver high-quality goods or services and provide top-notch customer support.

For people wishing to launch a business or supplement their income, e-commerce can be a tempting multiple source of income. E-commerce offers a great profit potential, the capacity to reach a large audience, and low administrative costs. To succeed in e-commerce, you must, nevertheless, plan carefully, market well, and offer high-quality goods or services.

## Social Media Management

With billions of users using social media platforms daily, social media has solidified its place as a fundamental component of contemporary life. As a result, managing social media has emerged as a popular method of creating various revenue streams. Creating and curating content, interacting with followers, tracking engagement metrics, and maintaining social media accounts for corporations or individuals are all part of social media management. Social media management involves managing and creating content for social media accounts (Vazquez, 2021

The flexibility that social media management provides is one of its key benefits. The ability to work remotely from anywhere in the world allows social media managers to juggle numerous sources of revenue. A social media manager, for instance, might handle a few social media accounts in the morning, work on creating social media strategies in the afternoon, and finish up another project in the evening.

The variety of opportunities offered is another benefit of social media management. Social media managers can work with a wide range of clients, including small businesses, multinational enterprises, and businesses in a variety of sectors, including technology, fashion, and beauty. As a result, they can diversify their sources of income and lower the risk associated with doing so.

Social media management can be financially rewarding depending on the sort of management and the client's budget. While some customers pay by the hour, others pay by the project. Additionally, social media managers can bargain their fees and charge extra for specialized services like influencer marketing, content development, or social media advertising.

Strong social media abilities, such as understanding of social media platforms, content development, and social media marketing tactics, are necessary for success as a social media manager. Also, social media administrators must be well-organized, possess outstanding communication abilities, and be able to handle several social media accounts at once. To locate clients, they can also sign up for social media management systems like Hootsuite, Sprout Social, or Buffer.

For those Gig workers who enjoy using social media and have the abilities and motivation to succeed, social media management can be a lucrative multiple stream of income. Flexibility, a variety of options, and the possibility for substantial income are all features of social media management. Nonetheless, a successful career in social media management involves effort, commitment, and perseverance.

## Kindle eBooks publishing on Amazon

In recent years, the popularity of eBooks has soared, and Amazon's Kindle platform has become one of the most popular and accessible platforms for self-publishing. Kindle Direct Publishing (KDP) allows anyone to publish their eBook on Amazon and start earning royalties from sales. In this essay, we will explore the benefits of using Kindle eBooks to make income and discuss how to use keywords on Amazon to advertise the book at low cost.

Firstly, using Kindle eBooks on Amazon provides an excellent opportunity for authors to publish their work and reach a broad audience. With KDP, authors can easily upload their manuscript, cover design, and description, and have their book available for purchase on Amazon within hours. The process is simple, free, and has no upfront costs. This means that even new authors or those on a tight budget can publish their work without having to invest in printing, distribution, or marketing.

Moreover, Kindle eBooks allow for flexibility in pricing, which can be a significant advantage for authors. Unlike traditional publishing, where the publisher determines pricing, authors can choose their pricing strategy on Kindle. They can set the price low to attract readers, or higher to earn more royalties per sale. Additionally, authors can enroll in KDP Select, which offers additional benefits such as access to promotional tools, and the ability to earn royalties from the Kindle Unlimited and Kindle Owners' Lending Library programs.

Using keywords on Amazon is an effective strategy for advertising the book at low cost. Keywords are the words or phrases that people use when searching for a specific product on Amazon. Authors can increase the book's visibility and attract more potential readers by including relevant keywords in the book's title, subtitle, and description. The key is to choose keywords specific to the book's genre and topic, with high search volume and low competition.

Amazon offers several tools to help authors find the right keywords. The first is the Amazon autocomplete feature, which suggests popular search terms as you type in the search bar. Another tool is the Amazon keyword tool, which provides a list of relevant keywords and their search volume. Additionally, authors can analyze their competitors' keywords by using tools such as Publisher Rocket, which can give insights into their competitors' keywords and their ranking on Amazon.

Using Kindle eBooks on Amazon is an excellent way for authors to publish their work and earn income. With KDP, authors have control over their pricing, and can reach a global audience quickly and easily. To advertise the book at low cost, authors should use relevant keywords in the book's title, subtitle, and description. By doing so, they can increase the book's visibility and attract more potential readers, leading to more sales and more income

Other Side hustles to consider

- Food delivery or courier services: Apps like Uber Eats, DoorDash, or Postmates allow you to earn money by delivering food or packages in your area.

- Pet sitting or dog walking: Many pet owners need reliable and trustworthy pet sitters or dog walkers. You can advertise your services on websites like Rover or Care.com.

- Personal shopping or styling: If you have an eye for fashion, you can offer personal shopping or styling services to help people update their wardrobe or find the perfect outfit for a special occasion.

- Airbnb hosting: If you have a spare room or apartment, you can rent it out on Airbnb to earn extra income.

- Handyman or home repair services: If you have home repair or maintenance skills, you can offer your services to homeowners in your area.

- Photography or videography: If you have a talent for photography or videography, you can offer your services for weddings or corporate events.

- Online surveys or product testing: Some websites like Swagbucks or InboxDollars offer paid online surveys or product testing opportunities.

These are just a few ideas for side hustles in 2023. The best side hustle for you will depend on your skills, interests, and availability. Choosing a side hustle that you enjoy and fits your schedule and financial goals is important.

## Entrepreneurship business skills

If you want to work in business, here are ten skills you will need.

1. Teamwork: Professional success is impossible without the ability to collaborate with others.

2. Creativity: Regardless of your area of expertise in the industry, the more creative you are, the easier it will be for you to find a profession in advertising.

3. People Skills: Even if you have exceptional people skills, working with a clientele likely to be very demanding will result in a high-stress level.

4. Problem-Solving: You can come up with an acceptable answer to any conundrum with the right problem-solving skills, but you need to act quickly.

5. Money Management: To succeed, you'll almost probably need to know how to work within a strict advertising budget.

6. Patience: Your marketing and advertising campaigns will always take time to elicit the desired response. An advertiser who is patient has a better chance of success.

7. Making decisions: Effective decisions require a balance between logic and imagination.

8. Persuasion: The main goal of advertising is to influence others to think as you want them to.

9. Time Management: You won't ever fulfill important deadlines to finish the project if you can't manage your own and other people's time.

10. Listening is one of the most powerful qualities you can have,

according to advertising professionals.

## Writing a business plan

You will need to write a business plan as you begin your new endeavor. A well-written business plan should contain information on your company's objectives, goods or services, and finances.

Your company's financial objectives are described in the business plan, along with the steps you will take to reach them. A comprehensive strategy will give the company a roadmap for the following three to five years, and you can share it with prospective investors, lenders, or other significant partners. To write your business strategy, follow these 9 steps:

1.  Write an executive summary

The first page of your company strategy is this one. Consider it your elevator speech. A purpose statement, a succinct rundown of the goods or services provided, and a general outline of your financial expansion strategies should all be included. Even though your investors will read the executive summary first, it may be simpler to write it last. By doing this, you may emphasize the data you've discovered when you write additional, more in-depth portions.

2.  Company description and details

According to Nerdwall.com, you will need to include your company description, which should contain information like the following (NerdWallet.com).

-   Your business's registered name.
-   Address of your business location.

- Names of key people in the business. Make sure to highlight unique skills or technical expertise among your team members.

Your company description should also specify the legal form of your firm, such as a sole proprietorship, partnership, or corporation, as well as the percentage of ownership and level of involvement that each owner has in the business.

Your firm's history and industry's current state should also be included. This gets the reader ready to read about your objectives in the following section.

3.  State your business goals

An objective statement comes in third place in a business strategy. This section outlines your short- and long-term goals in great detail.

If you're requesting a business loan or outside investment, you can use this part to explain why you need the money, how it will help your firm expand, and how you plan to fulfill your growth goals. The key is ensuring everyone is aware of the opportunities and how the loan or investment will aid in business expansion.

For instance, if your business is creating a second product line, you could explain how the loan will assist you launch the new line and how much you think sales will increase over the next three years.

4.  Describe your products and services

In this section, provide specifics about the goods or services you intend to provide.

You ought to incorporate the following:

- A description of your product or service's operation.

- Your product or service's pricing structure.

- The typical clients you deal with.

- Your approach to order fulfillment and your supply chain.

- Your sales plan.

- Your plan for distribution.

You can also talk about the registered or pending trademarks and patents associated with your good or service.

5. Do your market research

Investors and lenders will be curious as to how your product differs from that of the competition. Identify your competitors in the market analysis part of your paper. Outline what you can do better while discussing what they do well. Explain if you're catering to a niche or underserved clientele..

6. Outline your marketing and sales plan

Here, you can discuss your strategies for convincing customers to purchase your goods or services or for cultivating client loyalty that will result in recurring business.

7. Perform a business financial analysis

If your business is a startup, you might not be very familiar with your finances. Even if your business is already up and running, you should still include income or profit-and-loss statements, a balance sheet that lists your assets and liabilities, and a cash flow statement that shows how cash is brought into and out of the company. Also, you could include indicators like:

- Net profit margin, which is the share of revenue that you keep as net income.

- Current ratio: used to gauge your liquidity and debt-paying capacity.

- Accounts receivable turnover ratio: a gauge of how frequently receivables are collected annually.

8. Make financial projections

This is a crucial part of any company strategy, whether you're seeking finance or investors. It explains how your business will generate enough revenue to cover the loan or how you'll give investors a fair return.

Here, you should forecast your company's monthly or quarterly revenues, expenses, and earnings over the following three years, assuming that you have obtained a new loan.

Review your prior financial accounts thoroughly before generating estimates since accuracy is crucial. Your goals should be challenging yet still reachable.

9. Add additional information to an appendix

Add any supplementary information or documents that you couldn't fit elsewhere, such the resumes of key personnel, licenses, equipment leases, permits, patents, receipts, bank statements, contracts, and credit histories for both personal and professional usage. If the appendix is lengthy, you might want to consider starting this section with a table of contents.

## Angel investing for seed money

When starting a new business, funding is often the biggest obstacle. One way to secure seed money is through angel investing. Angel investing is the process of receiving capital from family and friends of the founder(s) and is often seen as a leap of faith. Since the company has no revenues or financial track record, exchanging money for equity is highly subjective. It relies heavily on trust and belief in the founders themselves by the angels.

Once entrepreneurs have fully utilized their potential angels, they may turn to non-institutional sources for capital in a pre-seed round of funding. Pre-seed rounds are typically not quite large enough for venture capital funds but are too big or beyond the resources of friends and family. According to company prospects and expectations, these rounds typically fall below the $250k level and may have a more structured approach to valuation and terms.

Angel and pre-seed funding is sometimes structured as SAFE (Simple Agreement for Future Equity) rounds, where the SAFE converts to equity only when the company raises its first priced round, as then it has actual metrics to come up with a fair valuation.

Once the small company has used all the angel and/or pre-seed funds and needs additional funding to sustain the business or keep up with early growth, they turn to the institutions and start talking to venture capital firms about Seed or Seed Series Funding.

Seed funding can be obtained from venture capital firms specializing in investing in early-stage companies and is usually used to fund product development and market research. Seed investors are looking for companies with great growth potential and return on investment. They will often invest in multiple companies at once, expecting only a few to succeed and provide a significant return on investment.

On the other hand, Series funding is typically provided by venture capital firms after a company has already shown some success and is looking to scale its operations. Series funding rounds are usually larger than seed rounds and help a company expand its market reach and increase its production capacity.

Angel investing is a great way for entrepreneurs to secure seed money for their businesses. With the support of family and friends, they can get the initial capital they need to start building their company. And once they have reached the limit of what angel and pre-seed funding can provide, they can turn to venture capital firms for additional funding to help them grow and scale their business. Any entrepreneur can turn their idea into a successful business with a solid business plan and the right support.

## Using Venture Capital to growing your business

Venture capital can be a powerful tool for entrepreneurs looking to grow their businesses. Venture capital refers to investments made by individuals or firms into high-growth companies that have the potential to yield significant returns. In exchange for their investment, venture capitalists typically receive an ownership stake in the company and a say in how it is run.

One of the key advantages of using venture capital to grow a business is the potential for significant funding. Venture capitalists are often willing to invest large amounts of capital into promising companies, which can provide the financial resources necessary to fuel growth and expansion. This funding can be precious for businesses in the early stages of development, as it can help them overcome early financial hurdles and build a strong foundation for future growth.

Another advantage of venture capital is the access to expertise and networks that investors can provide. Many venture capitalists have experience and connections in specific industries or markets and can provide valuable guidance and support to entrepreneurs. This can include advice on business strategy, introductions to potential partners or customers, and connections to other investors or resources.

However, using venture capital also comes with potential downsides. Venture capitalists typically expect significant returns on their investments, which can pressure entrepreneurs to prioritize growth over profitability. Additionally, venture capitalists often have a say in how the company is run, which can limit the freedom of entrepreneurs to make decisions that align with their vision for the business.

Using venture capital can be an effective way for entrepreneurs to grow their businesses. Venture capitalists can provide significant funding and valuable expertise and networks, which can help businesses overcome early hurdles and achieve their growth potential. However, entrepreneurs should carefully consider the potential downsides of using venture capital and ensure they are comfortable with the trade-offs involved. Ultimately, the decision to use venture capital should be based on the specific needs and goals of the business.

Venture capital firms are often structured as limited partnerships, or pools of capital, with the mandate to invest in early-stage companies.

These pools of capital include the venture capitalists' capital and capital from outside investors who are charged fees for management and performance.

In exchange for their investment, venture capitalists are given equity ownership in the companies they invest in and often have a seat or seats on the company's Board of Directors. They typically have specialized knowledge and expertise in the industries they invest in and can provide valuable advice and guidance on financial efficiency, growth, and operational risk management to their portfolio companies. This expertise gives them an advantage in investing and negotiating for equity ownership and board seats.

The amount of equity that venture firms receive for their investment is determined by several factors, including the amount of capital already invested in the company by the founders and their friends and family through angel and pre-seed funding. Overall, venture capital firms can provide critical funding, expertise, and guidance to early-stage companies, helping them overcome challenges and achieve their growth potential.

## Peer-to-peer lending

Peer-to-peer lending has revolutionized the way people invest their money. With the advent of online platforms, lending money to individuals and businesses has become easier than ever. Peer-to-peer lending provides a unique opportunity for investors to earn a passive income stream while helping others achieve their financial goals.

One of the most attractive aspects of peer-to-peer lending is the potential for higher returns than traditional investment options.

While stocks and bonds may offer modest returns, peer-to-peer lending can provide an average return of 5%-8% per year, depending on the platform and the risk level of the loans. This can be a great way to diversify your investment portfolio and increase your overall returns.

Another advantage of peer-to-peer lending is that it allows investors to choose their level of risk. Online platforms typically offer a range of loans with different risk levels, from low-risk loans with lower returns to higher-risk loans with potentially higher returns. This allows investors to tailor their investments to their risk tolerance and investment goals.

In addition, peer-to-peer lending is a relatively passive form of income. Once you have selected your loans and invested your money, the platform collects payments and distributes your earnings. This means you can earn money without actively managing your investments daily.

Overall, peer-to-peer lending can be a great investment option for those looking for a steady stream of passive income. By lending money to individuals and businesses, investors can earn attractive returns while helping others achieve their financial goals. As with any investment, it is important to research and choose a reputable platform that aligns with your investment goals and risk tolerance.

## Resources for Entrepreneurs

Starting a business can be an exciting and rewarding endeavor, but it can also be challenging, especially for those new to entrepreneurship. Fortunately, there are a variety of free resources available to entrepreneurs that can provide guidance, support, and valuable information. Two of these resources are the Small Business Administration (SBA) and SCORE.

The Small Business Administration (SBA) is a federal agency established to support and promote small businesses in the United States. One of the key services that the SBA provides is access to funding, including loans and grants. The SBA also offers free resources and support to entrepreneurs, including counseling, training, and guidance on starting and growing a business. This can be particularly helpful for new entrepreneurs unfamiliar with the legal, financial, and operational aspects of starting and running a business.

Another valuable resource for entrepreneurs is SCORE, which stands for Service Corps of Retired Executives. SCORE is a nonprofit organization that provides free mentoring, education, and resources to entrepreneurs. SCORE volunteers are retired executives and business owners who offer their expertise and experience to help entrepreneurs succeed. SCORE offers a range of resources, including workshops, webinars, online courses, and personalized mentoring. SCORE can provide valuable guidance and support if you need help with marketing, finances, operations, or other business aspects.

In addition to the SBA and SCORE, there are a variety of other free resources available to entrepreneurs. These may include local business development centers, community organizations, online forums, and communities. By taking advantage of these resources, entrepreneurs can gain valuable insights, make connections, and receive the support they need to succeed.

Starting a business can be challenging but rewarding, and various free resources are available to help entrepreneurs along the way. The

Small Business Administration and SCORE are excellent resources that offer entrepreneurs valuable guidance, support, and resources. By taking advantage of these and other resources, entrepreneurs can gain the knowledge and support they need to start and grow a successful business.

# CHAPTER 13: DEBT MANAGEMENT AND CREDIT MASTERY

## STRATEGIES FOR FINANCIAL STABILITY

"Interest on debts grows without rain."
**—Yiddish Proverb**

My friend John sat at his desk, staring at the stack of bills before him. He knew he was deep in financial debt but wasn't about to give up. John had been a fighter ever since he was a young boy growing up on the streets of east L.A. He learned to take whatever life threw at him and turn it into an opportunity. And now, he was determined to do the same with his debt.

He spent the next few weeks pouring over every financial document he could get his hands on. He studied the stock market, read books on investing, and even took a few online courses. Slowly but surely,

John began to see a way out of his mess. He began to invest his money wisely, making intelligent decisions and taking calculated risks.

It wasn't easy, and there were times when he felt like giving up. But he knew he couldn't. He had to keep fighting, no matter how hard it got. And finally, John did it after a couple of years of hard work and determination. He paid off all his debts and was finally free. As he sat back in his chair, looking at the city below, he knew this was only the beginning. He had proven he could accomplish anything he set his mind to and was ready to take on the world.

## The Current Condition of Debt in the U.S.

Now, let's take a look at the U.S. budget. The US government spends money on things like defense, health care, education, and helping people in need. To pay for these programs, the government takes money from its citizens in the form of taxes and sells bonds to borrow money.

The debt budget things were not looking good for the US budget even before the COVID-19 pandemic. The country already had a big deficit, which means that it spent more money than it brought in through taxes. This deficit was paid for by borrowing money, which added to the macro debt of the country.

But since the pandemic hit, the US government has issued a lot of debt to pay for economic stimulus programs and keep the economy going. Because of this, the US's overall debt situation has gotten worse today.

This means a lot for how the US economy will do in the future.

When there is a lot of debt, interest rates can go up, making it more expensive for the government and for people to borrow money. It can also cause inflation and the dollar's value to decrease.

The USdebtclock is an online real-time display of various economic data related to the United States, including the national debt, budget deficits, government spending, tax revenue, population, and other economic indicators. It was created to visually represent the US economy's current state and promote awareness of its financial situation.

The USdebtclock updates these figures continuously and estimates the country's total debt and future projections based on various economic factors. It also provides a breakdown of the debt per citizen and a comparison to other countries.

The USdebtclock is often used by economists, journalists, and politicians to monitor the country's financial health and to inform public policy debates. However, some critics argue that the display of the national debt and other economic data can be misleading or overly simplistic and does not consider the complexities of the global economy.

You can go to https://www.usdebtclock.org/ to get the latest US budget figures. As you see in the chart from 2023 below, it wasn't looking all that great before. But now that the US has issued massive amounts of debt in the last few years, it's even much worse today.

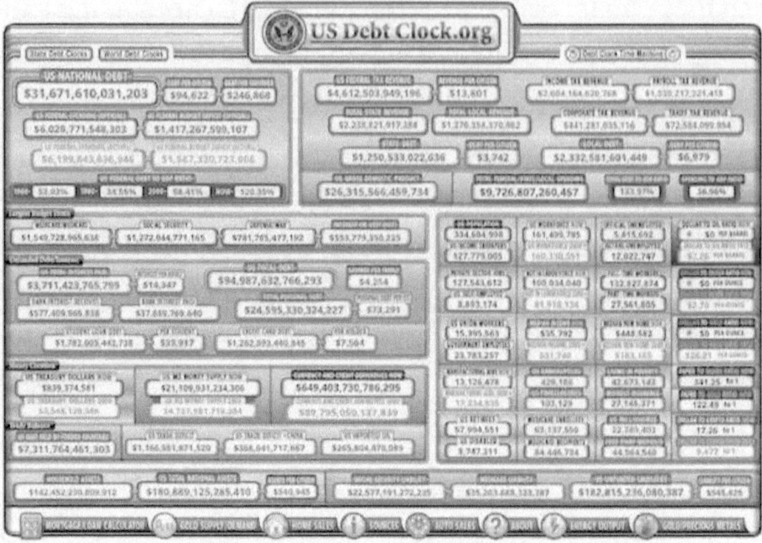

*Figure 14 (Source: USDebtClock.org).*

The current running total of US federal debt is $30.6 T, and US GDP is $ 26.3 T.

So just how much is a trillion dollars if you stacked them up by $100 bills? See the chart below.

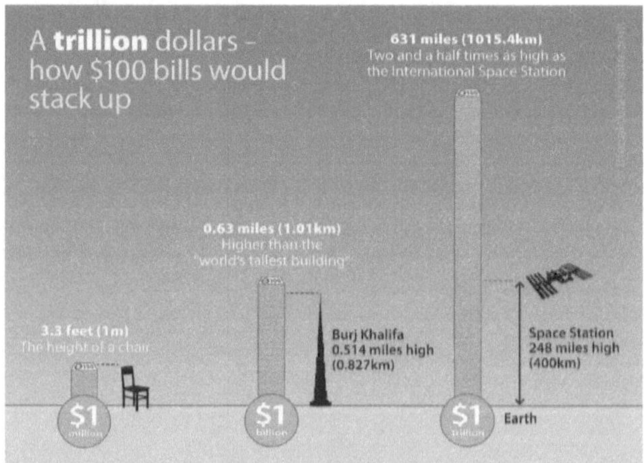


*Figure 15: Stacking a trillion dollars*

## What can we do to protect ourselves?

Our financial system is based on borrowing and debt. These debts eventually become unmanageable, even for the United States. The time will come when the hens must roost. There is just no way out for sovereigns as long as the US continues down this path of fiat manipulation and QE infinity, kicking the debt can down the road. Every single fiat-based national currency will eventually collapse under the weight of its obligations, whether it takes 10 years or 50.

The book's purpose is for you to grow multiple income streams. It is also prudent to allocate a portion of an investment portfolio to hard assets like gold and silver and a small percentage (1–5%) to major cryptocurrencies such as Bitcoin.

## Protecting and improving your credit report

According to balance.com, some employers, landlords, and insurance firms use credit scores to make decisions about job applications, potential tenants, and policyholders. Lenders use credit ratings to assist the estimation of the risk associated with borrowers (the Balance).

Your credit score can either save you money on loans or cost you money. Therefore the first step in building a strong credit profile is to understand your score.

Your credit report is one of your life's most important financial documents. It tells potential lenders, employers, and landlords how responsible you are with your money. A good credit report can open doors to new opportunities, while a bad one can slam them shut. Let me share a story of how a bad credit report can affect you and steps to fix and improve your FICO score.

Jane had always been responsible with her money. She paid her bills on time, had no credit card debt, and had never missed a payment. But one day, she received a letter in the mail from her bank. They checked her credit report and found a mistake. It said she had missed some payment on her credit card. Jane was shocked. She knew she had never missed a payment. But the mistake was there, and it was hurting her credit score.

Jane soon discovered that this credit report mistake affected her more than she thought. She was turned down for a new credit card and could not get a reasonable interest rate on a car loan. Even worse, when she applied for a new job, the employer checked her credit report and saw the mistake. They assumed she was irresponsible with her finances, and they didn't hire her.

Determined to fix her credit report, Jane took some steps to improve her FICO score. First, she contacted the credit reporting agency and disputed the error. She also requested a copy of her credit report to review for other mistakes. She then made sure to pay all her bills on time and to keep her credit card balance low. Over time, her credit score improved, and the mistake was corrected.

The moral of Jane's story is that your credit report affects you more than you think. A bad credit score can hurt your chances of getting a loan, a job, or even a place to live. But there are steps you can take to fix and improve your FICO score. Start by reviewing your credit report and disputing any mistakes. Then, pay your bills on time and keep your credit card balance low. Over time, your credit score will improve, and you'll be better positioned to take advantage of new opportunities.

Based on your past behavior with credit accounts, your credit score indicates how likely it is that you will repay a loan. The five main components of credit scoring—payment history, debt level, length of credit history, categories of credit, and most recent credit applications—are used to calculate a three-digit score using your credit history.

## Five reasons you should check your credit report:

1. It can aid in error detection and dispute. One in four persons is able to spot possible mistakes

2. Other people's errors could have an impact on your credit.

3. Prevent credit card fraud and identity theft early on.

4. Conserve cash by taking control of your credit.

5. Maintain a solid credit standing.

Good credit scores are preferable and show a history of good behavior, including timely bill payment, responsible use of available credit, and avoidance of bad behavior, such as late payments more than 30 days past due, accounts going to collections, and bankruptcy. On the other hand, lenders are more risk averse and charge higher interest rates to approve customers with lower scores because they have historically had problems making payments.

As your credit history ages and you add positive information, negative information often has less of an impact on your credit score. The majority of bad information won't impact your credit score after seven years.

There are numerous credit scoring models available, and each has a mechanism for figuring out your score. There are two well-known brands of scoring models: VantageScore and FICO.

## Understanding Credit Score Ranges

Most credit scores range from 300 to 850, with an 850 representing a perfect credit score. The higher your credit score, the better your credit. In general, credit scores fall in the following ranges:

- Below 580: Poor
- 580 to 669: Fair
- 670 to 739: Good
- 740 to 799: Very Good
- Above 800: Exceptional

Some credit scoring models may use a slightly different range, but higher scores will always be better.

## What a Good Credit Score Can Do for You

Beyond sheer vanity, having a high or good credit score has advantages. A high score makes it easier to qualify for lower interest rates, higher credit limits, larger loan amounts, and easier approval for credit cards and loans.

Several insurance companies will include your score when calculating your insurance rate. As a result, you can get insurance for less money if you have good credit than if you don't.

Cell phone stores are now on the list of companies that use your credit score. While smartphones often cost more than $1,000, paying for a phone in installments is economical. Your credit score determines whether and how much of a new phone you may finance through your carrier. You might be able to finance the phone of your choice with little or no down payment if you have good credit.

## How to Get Your Credit Score

Your credit score can be found from a variety of sources using data from your credit report. First, sites like Credit Karma let you check your score for free. Some banks, credit unions, and credit card companies may display your credit score online or on your billing statement.

Last point: Equifax, Experian, and TransUnion are the three main credit bureaus where you may view your credit score.

Several firms that supply your credit score will also include a gauge that allows you to decide whether you have good or terrible credit and the elements that affect your credit score in order to help you understand your score.

The data used to determine your credit score is in your credit report. Due to the financial difficulties brought on by the global pandemic, you can now obtain a free copy of your credit report every year from AnnualCreditReport.com.

## Credit score components

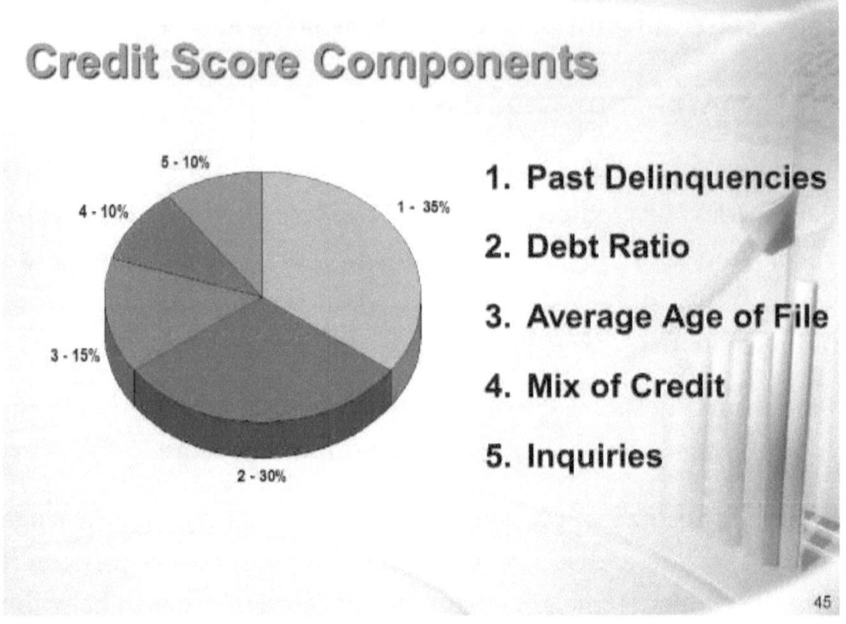


*Figure 16: Credit Score Components*

## How to Build Your Credit Score

To benefit from having high credit, there are many strategies to raise your credit score. Making on-time payments on existing credit cards or loans would assist a lot because your credit score is largely influenced by your payment history, which accounts for 35% of your credit score.

Maintaining a healthy balance on your credit cards is crucial because 30% of your credit score is based on your debt, including your balances on those cards.

The debt calculations that account for 30% of your score heavily depend on your credit utilization, which shows how much of your available credit you really utilize. You would have $9,000 in accessible credit, for instance, if you had three credit cards with $3,000 maximums each. Keep your balances below 30% of your credit limits as a basic rule of thumb.

As 15% of your credit score is determined by how long you've had credit, the earlier you start improving your credit score, the better. Your credit age will be low when you first start using credit, but as you acquire expertise, having accounts that are well-established will raise the average age of your funds.

Consider getting a secured credit card if you have no credit history and no open accounts. This account is simpler to start for those who are new to credit, but it does require a security deposit as collateral for the credit line.

Conversely, a friend or member of your family with strong credit may add you as an authorized user to their account. By doing this, you'll gain access to their whole credit history, which could be useful when you apply for credit.

Tips to improve your credit score

1.  Pay your bills on time every time

2.  Don't get close to your credit limit

3.  Long credit history will help your score

4.  Only apply for credit that you need

5.  Check your credit report regularly and make sure the information is correct at AnnualCreditReport.com

6.  Dispute anything that shows up as questionable on your report

## How Interest Rates Affect You

Interest rates play a crucial role in our daily lives, impacting our ability to borrow money, save for the future, and make critical financial decisions. Understanding how interest rates affect us is essential for making informed financial choices and achieving financial security.

Interest rates are the cost of borrowing money, and they fluctuate based on various economic factors, including inflation, supply and demand, and government policy. When interest rates are low, borrowing money becomes cheaper, making it easier for individuals to obtain loans for big-ticket items like homes and cars. Low-interest rates can also encourage consumer spending, as people feel more confident about purchasing without incurring high-interest charges.

On the other hand, high interest rates can make borrowing money more expensive, limiting credit availability and slowing economic growth. Savings accounts and other interest-bearing investments may yield lesser returns at high interest rates, which can make saving money more difficult.

Interest rates can also impact the value of different assets, such as stocks and bonds. When interest rates are low, investors may be more likely to invest in stocks, as they can offer higher returns than low-yield bonds. Conversely, when interest rates are high, bonds may become more attractive, offering higher returns than stocks.

Interest rates may also affect currency exchange rates, as higher interest rates can attract foreign investment and increase demand for a country's currency. This can impact international trade and investment and impact the global economy as a whole.

In addition to their impact on the economy, interest rates can significantly impact our finances. For example, credit card interest rates can impact our ability to pay off debt. In contrast, mortgage interest rates can impact our ability to purchase a home or refinance an existing mortgage. Interest rates can also impact the value of our retirement accounts, as high-interest rates can boost investment returns, while low-interest rates can limit growth potential.

Interest rates play a significant role in our financial lives, impacting our ability to borrow, save, and invest. Understanding how interest rates affect us is essential for making informed financial decisions and achieving long-term financial security. By staying informed about interest rate trends and seeking professional advice when needed, we can make the most of our financial resources and achieve our financial goals.

## Credit card debt:

Credit card debt can be a source of stress and financial burden for many individuals. High-interest rates and fees can make it challenging to pay off balances, and the cycle of debt can seem never-ending. The highest interest rate that a credit card company can legally charge varies depending on the country and state or province. In the United States, for example, the maximum interest rate that credit card companies can charge is regulated by each state. The maximum rate is typically around 25-30% APR (annual percentage rate). However, some credit cards may have penalty APRs that can be as high as 29.99% for late payments or going over your credit limit. It's important to read the terms and conditions of your credit card agreement carefully to understand the interest rates and fees associated with your account. The fact that credit card companies can charge such a high fee should be a crime. With discipline and a clear plan, it is possible to eliminate personal credit card debt and regain financial freedom.

The first step in eliminating credit card debt is to stop adding to it. It's important to assess your spending habits and identify any unnecessary expenses that can be cut back. This can involve creating a budget, tracking expenses, and prioritize essential expenses. You can redirect those funds toward paying off your credit card balances by reducing spending.

Next, it's important to prioritize your debts. This involves listing your credit card debts from highest to lowest interest rate and focusing on paying off the highest interest rate balances first. This strategy, known as the "debt avalanche" method, can help you save money in interest charges over time and reduce the overall amount of debt you owe.

Another effective strategy for eliminating credit card debt is to consolidate your debts. This involves transferring high-interest balances to a credit card with a lower interest rate or taking out a personal loan to pay off your credit card balances. By consolidating your debts, you can reduce your interest charges and make it easier to manage your payments.

It's also important to make regular payments towards your credit card debts. This involves making the minimum payments on all your credit cards and allocating extra funds towards your highest interest rate balances. By making regular payments, you can reduce the interest you owe and make progress toward paying off your debts.

Finally, seeking professional help can be a valuable strategy for eliminating credit card debt. This can involve working with a credit counseling agency or a financial advisor who can guide managing your debts and creating a repayment plan. These professionals can also negotiate with creditors on your behalf and help you reduce your interest rates and fees.

Making it a priority to eliminate your personal credit card debt can be challenging, but with discipline and a clear plan, it is possible to regain financial freedom. By reducing your spending, prioritizing your debts, consolidating your debts, making regular payments, and seeking professional help, you can take control of your finances and eliminate your credit card debt for good.

Since the Federal Reserve raised interest rates, short-term debts like credit cards, auto, and home equity lines of credit have experienced an increase in rates, resulting in higher interest payments. Additionally, those with adjustable-rate mortgages may face higher monthly mortgage payments. If you're feeling financially burdened by these rate hikes, seeking advice from a mortgage or wealth manager professional may help alleviate the pressure. They can guide you through possible options to ease the financial strain.

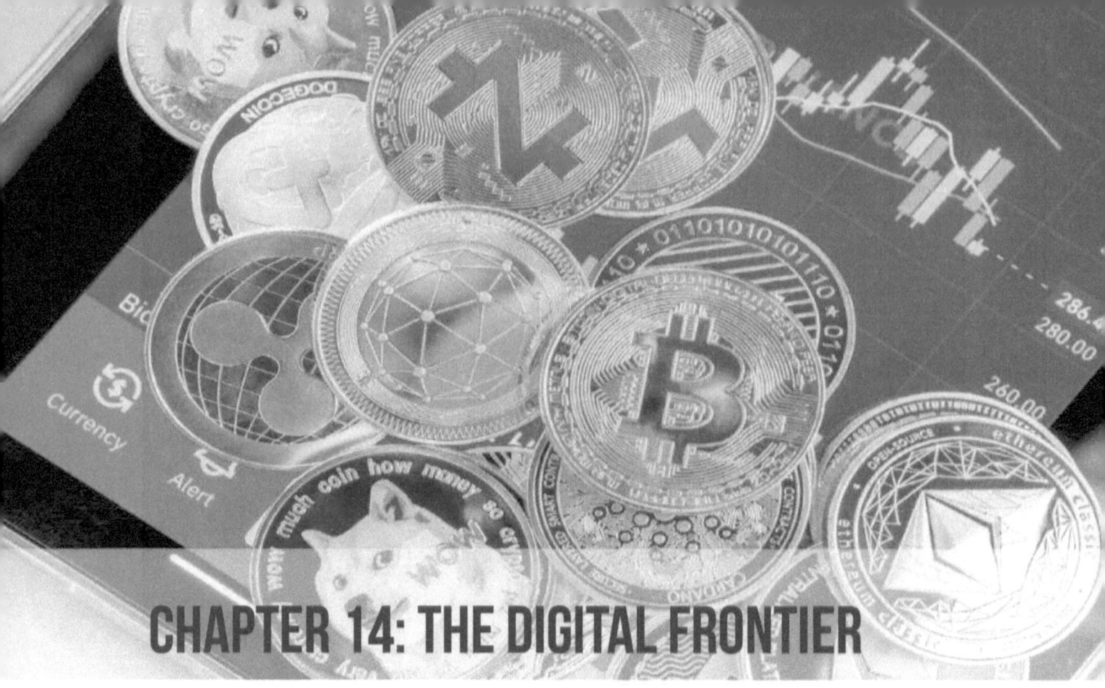

# CHAPTER 14: THE DIGITAL FRONTIER

## CRYPTO ASSETS AND THE FUTURE OF INVESTING

---

"Innovation distinguishes between a leader and a follower." —**Steve Jobs**

---

It was another hot summer day in Southern California. A group of tech enthusiasts gathered in a conference room at the campus. Among them was Ben, a professor, young stats teacher, and investor with a passion for digital technology and cryptocurrency. He had been following the industry for years, and he knew that there was a tremendous opportunity to be found in this space.

As the meeting began, we spoke about the latest trends in the industry, highlighting the rise of blockchain technology and its potential for the future of finance. Ben leaned in, his eyes sparkling excitedly as he listened intently to the other professors. He knew this was the future and was determined to be a part of it.

Over the next few months, Ben poured his heart and soul into his investments, carefully selecting the best digital assets and cryptocurrencies to add to his portfolio. He spent countless hours researching and analyzing each investment, always looking for the next big opportunity. And then, one day, it happened. One of Ben's investments exploded in value, skyrocketing to unprecedented heights. He had struck gold and knew this was only the beginning.

Over the next few years, Ben's investments in digital technology and cryptocurrency continued to pay off, providing him with financial freedom and security that he had never imagined possible. He watched with pride as the industry continued to grow and evolve, bringing new and exciting developments to finance.

But despite celebrating his success, Ben never lost sight of the bigger picture. He knew that his investments were not just a way to make money but a way to help shape the future of finance and technology. He was proud to be a part of a movement that was changing the world, one digital asset at a time.

And so, as the years went by, Ben continued to invest in digital technology and cryptocurrency, constantly pushing himself to find new and innovative ways to make a difference in the world. He knew that the future was bright, and he was excited to be a part of it. The sky was the limit for Ben, and he was determined to soar.

## Let's Start With What Is Money

Money is a means of economic exchange in today's world. It is a good that is widely regarded as acceptable. It has to do with the medium used to represent values and prices. It is how we track our money and circulate from person to person and country to country, promoting trade between nations. Money is anything that people accept in exchange for goods and services. Money serves as our country's currency in modern economies.

## Money has the following main characteristics:

1.  Money is a medium of trade because it is used to buy and sell things. It makes it easier for buyers and sellers to do business with each other by letting people trade goods and services for a form of money that everyone knows and accepts.

2.  Money is also used as a unit of account, which means it is a standard way to measure the value of things and services. Money makes it easy to compare and figure out how much different goods and services are worth in a consistent way.

3.  Money can also be used as a store of value, which means that it can be saved and used to buy things in the future. When money is saved or invested, it can make interest or go up in value, which helps people get richer over time.

4.  Money is easy to move around, which makes it easy for people to carry and trade. This is especially important in the modern economy, where people often travel long distances to do work or to visit family.

5.  Money is also divisible, which means that it can be split into smaller amounts of value. This lets people buy and sell things of all kinds, from small items to big investments.

6.  Durable: Money is made to last and last for a long time. It is made of materials that don't wear out easily, and it is often made so that it is hard to fake.

In our modern economy, money needs to have these traits in order to work well as a way to buy things, keep track of money, and store worth. If we understand these things about money, we can better understand how important it is to our lives and to the business as a whole

The cryptocurrency does have some of the same features as a fiat currency system. It is hard to get, and it can't be faked. Bitcoin is a new species that is much better than the ones that came before it. Below, we go into more detail about these differences between different kinds of money.

| Money Traits | Fiat Money | Gold | Crypto (Bitcoin) |
|---|---|---|---|
| Decentralized | Low | Low | High |
| Divisable | Medium | Medium | High |
| Durable | Medium | High | High |
| Easy to Transact | High | Low | High |
| Fungible | High | High | High |
| Non Consumable | High | High | High |
| Portability | High | Medium | High |
| Programable | Low | Low | High |
| Scarce | Low | Low | High |
| Secure | Medium | Medium | High |
| Sovereign | High | Medium | Low |

*Table 1: Traits of Money*

## FDR Takes the United States off the Gold Standard

The United States exited the gold standard, a monetary system in which currency is backed by gold, when Congress enacted a joint resolution removing creditors' right to demand payment in gold on June 5, 1933 (FDR Takes United States Off Gold Standard - HISTORY). This Day in History (https://www.history.com).

In order to tackle the country's inflation problem and discourage foreign governments from exchanging ever-increasing amounts of dollars for gold, President Richard Nixon closed the gold window later, in 1971.

Banks and the US government have been the principal creators of new US dollars through the issuing of loans and coins, respectively, since 1971, when the gold connection was severed. Nothing is therefore left to "support" the US dollar. This is referred to as Fiat money. The Latin word "fiat," which means an authoritative judgment, is where the term "fiat currency" originates. In this case, the U.S. government establishes the value of the currency, which is not a representation of any other asset or financial instrument, such as gold or a check. When President Nixon ruled that the US Dollar could no longer be turned into gold, this historic moment heralded the end of the US Dollar's gold backing.

## Introducing Bitcoin as the New Digital Currency

Bitcoin is a digital currency that was created in 2009. It is a decentralized currency, meaning that any government or financial institution does not control it. Bitcoin uses a technology called blockchain to record transactions, which is highly secure and transparent.

Many people have invested in Bitcoin, and there are various opinions about whether it is a good investment. Some people believe Bitcoin is a good investment because it is a digital asset not tied to any government or institution, making it more resistant to inflation and economic instability. Others believe that Bitcoin is a risky investment because it is highly volatile, meaning its value can fluctuate greatly over short periods.

Whether or not Bitcoin is a good investment depends on several factors, including an individual's investment goals, risk tolerance, and overall financial situation. Additionally, it is important to consider that the cryptocurrency market, including Bitcoin, is largely unregulated and can be subject to significant price fluctuations.

As for whether it is too late to invest in Bitcoin, there is no clear answer. Some people believe that the cryptocurrency market is still in its early stages and that there is potential for growth in the future, while others believe that the market is already saturated and that Bitcoin's value may have peaked.

When deciding how much money to invest in Bitcoin, it is important to remember that any investment comes with risks. It is generally recommended that individuals only invest money they can afford to lose and diversify their investments across a range of assets to reduce their overall risk.

## Bitcoin Cycles

The cycles of Bitcoin are based on supply and demand, and the market is largely driven by investor sentiment. There is also a 4-year cycle of Bitcoin, known as the "halving cycle," refers to the regular pattern in which the rate at which new Bitcoin is created, called the block reward, which is cut in half every four years. This process is a key part of Bitcoin's design, intended to gradually reduce the rate of new Bitcoin entering circulation until the maximum supply of

21 million Bitcoin is reached.

The halving events occur approximately every four years, and they are programmed into the Bitcoin network's code. Specifically, every 210,000 blocks, the block reward is reduced by half. The initial block reward was 50 BTC per block, but after the first halving in 2012, it was reduced to 25 BTC. After the second halving in 2016, it was further reduced to 12.5 BTC, and after the third halving in 2020, it was reduced to 6.25 BTC.

The 4-year cycle is significant because it has historically been accompanied by a surge in Bitcoin's price. This is because the reduction in the rate of new Bitcoin entering circulation reduces the selling pressure on the market, making it easier for demand to drive up the price. Additionally, the halving events are often seen as a validation of Bitcoin's scarcity and long-term value proposition.

Bitcoin has experienced several boom-and-bust cycles over the years, with periods of rapid growth followed by sharp declines in value. These cycles can be challenging to predict and are influenced by various factors, including changes in government regulations, news events, and the overall economic climate.

Last but not least, the people or individuals who invented Bitcoin go by the moniker Satoshi Nakamoto. Although though Satoshi Nakamoto's exact identity is still a mystery, their contributions to the creation of Bitcoin and the blockchain technology that underpins it are largely regarded as ground-breaking developments in the field of digital currency.

In 2008, the mysterious Satoshi released the well-known Bitcoin whitepaper outlining the technical details and goals of the cryptocurrency. In the essay, Satoshi makes the case that Bitcoin is a compelling example of why a new online payment system should be created.

## A new coin is created

With a peer-to-peer version of electronic cash, online payments might be done directly from one party to another without going through a banking organization. Digital signatures help with the problem in some ways, but the main benefits are lost if a trustworthy third party is still required to prevent double-spending. We propose a peer-to-peer network to address the problem of double spending. By hashing transactions into an ongoing chain of hash-based proof-of-work, the network timestamps transactions and creates a record that cannot be changed without repeating the proof-of-work. The longest chain provides both proof that the events occurred as they were observed and proof that it came from the most CPU power. As long as the bulk of the CPU power is retained by nodes that are not cooperating to attack the network, they will create the longest chain and surpass attackers. For the network itself, hardly much structure is required. Nodes are free to join and quit the network whenever they like, using the longest proof-of-work chain as verification of what happened while they were gone. Messages are disseminated with all due diligence.

## What leaders are saying about the future of Bitcoin

Bitcoin, the world's first decentralized digital currency, has been in the spotlight for the past decade (Fidelity, 2023). Despite initial skepticism, Bitcoin has proven to be a game-changer in the world of finance, and legislators, CEOs, and thought leaders are taking note of its potential. Many of these individuals have been vocal in their support of Bitcoin and have made some compelling and positive statements about its future.

One of the most prominent supporters of Bitcoin is Jack Dorsey, the CEO of Twitter and Square. Dorsey has long been a vocal proponent of Bitcoin and has publicly stated that he believes it will eventually become the world's "single currency." In fact, Square, the mobile payments company he founded, recently invested $50 million in Bitcoin, stating that it believes the cryptocurrency has the potential to become a "more ubiquitous currency in the future."

Another high-profile CEO who has expressed support for Bitcoin is Elon Musk, the CEO of Tesla and SpaceX. Although he has been somewhat controversial in his statements about cryptocurrency, Musk has recently made it clear that he believes in Bitcoin's potential. In a recent interview, he stated that he believes Bitcoin is "a good thing" and that he has personally invested in the cryptocurrency.

Legislators have also been taking notice of Bitcoin's potential. Senator Cynthia Lummis of Wyoming has been a vocal proponent of Bitcoin and other cryptocurrencies in the United States. She has strongly advocated for legislation supporting the growth and development of the crypto industry, stating that she believes Bitcoin is "a great store of value."

Similarly, in El Salvador, the government recently made Bitcoin legal tender, making it the first country in the world to do so. President Nayib Bukele has stated that he believes Bitcoin can help to promote financial inclusion and reduce the country's dependence on the US dollar.

Thought leaders in finance have also been weighing in on Bitcoin's potential. Michael Saylor, the CEO of MicroStrategy, has become one of the most prominent supporters of Bitcoin in the business world.

His company has invested billions of dollars in cryptocurrency, and Saylor has publicly stated that he believes it is the "most dominant monetary network on the planet."

Ray Dalio, the billionaire investor and founder of Bridgewater Associates, has also expressed support for Bitcoin. While he has acknowledged that he does not fully understand cryptocurrency, he has stated that he believes it could become an "alternative store of wealth" if it continues to gain acceptance and adoption.

In conclusion, the future of Bitcoin looks bright, with support coming from legislators, CEOs, and thought leaders worldwide. While there is still some skepticism and uncertainty surrounding cryptocurrency, many believe that it has the potential to revolutionize the world of finance and become a dominant force in the global economy. As more and more people continue to embrace Bitcoin, its future looks brighter than ever.

## So, what exactly is Bitcoin?

The initial kind of decentralized digital money is called Bitcoin, or BTC. Considering that it is decentralized, which means that no business, bank, government, or other organization supports, oversees, or owns it. Instead, Bitcoin is controlled by computer software that anybody with an internet connection may download and use to track and validate transactions (Fidelity.2023). (To put it in perspective, the US government supports the dollar and is governed by the US Federal Reserve.

The digital token (sometimes called Bitcoin) sits on a distributed network of computers. The currency is solely produced digitally rather than on paper like the dollar. As a result, it cannot be taken out of its digital network and does not have a physical existence like paper money. Physical Bitcoins cannot be inserted into wallets. This is still true even if you purchase your Bitcoin from an ATM.

## How does Bitcoin work?

A blockchain is the computer code and technology that underpins Bitcoin and all other cryptocurrencies (Fidelity.2023). You might think of a blockchain as a sizable digital database, or ledger, that collects and distributes all the information about each and every

Bitcoin transactions to machines that are running the Bitcoin software over the internet (Fidelity, 2023). Each cryptocurrency has a distinct blockchain that is particular to it. In order to create a chain utilizing cryptographic operations, the computers running the program organize transactions into blocks, which are subsequently added to the database or ledger in a particular order. As a result, they introduced "blockchain" and "cryptocurrency." There are thousands of nodes, which are computers that operate the Bitcoin software.

Since Bitcoin is a digital currency, it may be used to conduct transactions and transfer funds internationally. Bitcoin is utilized as a store of value and as an investment (Fidelity, 2023).

## Where does Bitcoin come from?

One mine Bitcoin. On the Bitcoin blockchain, new transactions are validated in this manner. New currencies are created or mined when computers on the network verify and process transactions. The transaction is processed by these networked computers, or miners, in return for a Bitcoin payment.

Bitcoin transactions are verified by miners, who compete with one another to solve cryptographic challenges. So, depending on how much you want to pay in fees and how certain you want to be that the transaction is properly confirmed, transactions can take anywhere from 10 to 60 minutes on average. Although this is far quicker than electronic fund transfers, which can take days to process, credit card transactions, which can take only a few seconds, are much faster. A Bitcoin miner can be anyone. Yet your chances of receiving a Bitcoin reward are minimal unless you have access to extremely fast and potent machines like ASICs (that's "application-specific integrated circuits").

In order to compensate miners for their committed computing resources and electricity used to protect the Bitcoin network by confirming transactions, bitcoin mining puts new bitcoin into circulation. In 2022, mining bitcoin remained an extremely lucrative endeavor. Almost $20 million worth of bitcoin is mined every day by bitcoin miners. Also, new coins are issued on a schedule that was built into their programming at the time of creation.

## How many Bitcoin are there?

Because there can never be more than 21 million Bitcoins, a finite number are available. However, given the software code of Bitcoin and the way the rules are upheld, it is highly improbable that this cap will be modified. More than 19 million Bitcoin have already been released out of the total of 21 million coins that will eventually be mined. It's also critical to be aware that the rate at which new Bitcoins are issued is roughly halved every four years; this is known as the halving.

Also, because to its high degree of divisibility, bitcoin can be purchased in very little quantities. A Satoshi, often known as "sat," is the smallest unit of the cryptocurrency Bitcoin. A Bitcoin can be divided to eight decimal places, which is more than most conventional currencies can. There are 100 million sats in a single bitcoin. Realizing that each Sat would be worth one cent if the price of a single Bitcoin were $1 million.

## Bitcoin's fundamental value proposition

Bitcoin offers a number of benefits. The first is that it resists seizures. The nature of Bitcoin transactions and the security safeguards in place make it practically hard for the authorities to freeze your assets. No national or regional government body has the ability to take your digital property. The security mechanisms built into bitcoin technology prevent unauthorized users from accessing your digital wallet.

Second, Bitcoin's supporters refer to it as "digital gold". The expression describes the notion that Bitcoin can act as a store of value similar to gold that is independent of other financial markets like stocks and bonds..

## How is Bitcoin's price determined?

Similar to the stock market, the price of stock shares, or the value of other currencies, supply and demand determine the price of bitcoin. The acceptance of Bitcoin by firms, governments, and investors, investor sentiment, the monetary policy of the central bank, inflation, and foreign exchange rates are a few variables that might affect supply and demand for Bitcoin.

Bitcoin's valuation as an investment has increased from $0.09 at its inception in 2009 to over $69,000 before declining to approximately

$15,800 in November 2022. As of mid April 2023 the price is around $30,124.

## How do we use Bitcoin?

Without using a middleman like a bank or credit card firm, people can transmit money to each other directly over the internet using Bitcoin. This transaction is referred to as a "peer-to-peer" one. If you presently use Venmo, PayPal, Cash App, or Zelle, you can conduct electronic transactions using conventional currencies using these apps. With Bitcoin, transfers can be made on the Bitcoin network using a smartphone app or online. Bitcoin, in contrast to those other providers of digital wallets, is a public system that is open to anyone globally.

## How to keep your Bitcoin safe

We employ Bitcoin wallets, a type of digital safe where you may store Bitcoin, to keep it secure. Your Bitcoin wallet will have a public address, similar to how your bank or investment account utilizes a routing number    (Fidelity.2023). It consists of what appear to be random letters and numbers that aren't always connected to names, locations, places of business, or other personally identifying details. To transmit, receive, and access their Bitcoin, the owner will need their public address as well as their public and private keys, which function similarly to passwords.

## Does Bitcoin charge any fees?

The platforms where users store their bitcoin will levy transaction fees to users who buy, sell, or move Bitcoin. Depending on the chosen funding channel, transaction expenses can range from

0.5% to 4%.

Also, each Bitcoin transaction involves a small network charge. The fee amount fluctuates depending on a number of variables and is automatically subtracted from the Bitcoin sent. Transaction costs on the core Bitcoin network fluctuate based on the network's congestion.

## Taxes on Bitcoin?

Sales or other dispositions of Bitcoin (and other cryptocurrencies) are often taxable events, just like any other stock, bond, or capital asset. Cryptocurrencies are not considered to be currencies by the IRS, but rather a sort of property (Fidelity.2023). You must pay income taxes on the current value of Bitcoin received as payment. You must pay taxes on the difference between the amount you paid for the cryptocurrency and the sale earnings if you sell it for a profit. In light of the short- and long-term holding period tax rules that are in place, the taxes on cryptocurrencies are thus comparable in many ways to those on other capital assets such as individual stocks and bonds. Be aware, nevertheless, that crypto taxes can be complicated. As an illustration, it would be safe to consult a tax expert if you are actively trading and making lots of crypto trades (Fidelity, 2023).

## Bitcoin investing risk

Trading Bitcoin has attracted a lot of people looking to earn a quick buck. You must use caution, though, as with other speculative investments. The dangers associated with purchasing, selling, and utilizing Bitcoin include:

1. Bitcoin's price has fluctuated greatly over the past 13 years. Most individuals find this volatility difficult, especially if they don't comprehend Bitcoin. Since 2009, Bitcoin has had 5 significant 80%+ declines. Six drawdowns of more than 50% have occurred. But, prudent investors overlook the short-term volatility and concentrate on the asset's long-term advantages. Investors may experience both substantial and sudden gains and losses. Bitcoin and other digital currencies have experienced unpredictable and significant price fluctuations.

2. Digital money like Bitcoin is not accepted as legal tender. Businesses or people have no legal requirement to accept Bitcoin as payment. Instead, only those people and companies accepting Bitcoin can utilize it. Also, cryptocurrency regulation is subject to change at any time, which could affect the outlook for investment in each cryptocurrency.

3. Bitcoin trading platforms are currently unregulated. Both have been and still might be hacked. Moreover, some have failed and others may quit functioning. Moreover, digital wallets are vulnerable to hacking, just like the platforms themselves. As a result, many consumers may lose a lot of money and already have.

4. Fraud and theft can occur in Bitcoin transactions. For instance, a scammer can pretend to be a Bitcoin exchange, middleman, or trader in order to persuade you to transmit money, which is then stolen (Fidelity, 2023).

5. If you lose the information needed to access your Bitcoin keys, you could lose them forever.

6. Unlike banking organizations, which are covered by FDIC

insurance, digital wallets are not similarly protected.

7. Bitcoin payments are designed to be irreversible (Fidelity, 2023). Once you complete a transaction, you cannot reverse it. Reversing a transaction depends solely on the willingness of the recipient to send back your Bitcoin.

It's crucial to consider your time horizon, financial situation, tolerance for volatility, and risk of loss while studying and assessing any investment. If you're considering investing in Bitcoin or opportunities similar to it, educate yourself on digital assets, be ready for huge price swings, and approach with extreme caution.

In January 2022, Consuelo Mack had an interview with renowned value investor Bill Miller for a Wealthtrack podcast. She questioned why he had put so much of his money into Bitcoin. His own investment portfolio now includes digital currency and a few associated crypto ventures, making up half of it. In the interview, Miller explains why he has changed from a self-described Bitcoin "watcher" to a Bitcoin "bull" and why he is increasing his holdings even though the price of the cryptocurrency has dropped by 60%. Bill Miller added the following justification for his belief in Bitcoin.

Many more countries, people, and venture capitalists' money is moving into Bitcoin.

- The thought of Bitcoin as digital gold and a store of value. Bitcoin, if held securely, cannot be confiscated. Miller stated that even in 1933, President Franklin D. Roosevelt confiscated everyone's gold in the US.

- Bitcoin is the only economic entity whose supply is unaffected by the demand. Therefore, only 21 million Bitcoin can only be created. From an economic standpoint, Bitcoin has a fixed supply of 21 million with growing demand. As opposed to the dollar, they are also known as fiat currency, where our government can continue to print the dollars. The federal government calls this quantitative easing (QE), in which a nation's central bank tries to increase the liquidity in its financial system by printing money to spur economic activity. However, this also results in inflation.

- Drawing parallels with the trajectory of historical technological advancements such as the printing press, railroads, automobiles, and electricity, Bill Miller closely observes the evolution of Bitcoin as a groundbreaking new technology.

- Bitcoin is an insurance policy against a financial catastrophe like what has happened in Venezuela.

I believe that to have the success you deserve, you need to create a strong foundation of knowledge of digital assets and cryptocurrencies. The list of well-to-do financial billionaire names who have bought Bitcoin includes Elon Musk, Paul Tudor Jones, Tim Draper, Chamath Palihapitiya, Ricardo Pleige, Michael Saylor, Tyler and Cameron Winklevoss, Sam Bankman-Fried, Changpeng Zhao, Jed McCaleb, Chris Larsen, Gary Wang, Song Chi-hyung, Barry Silbert, Fred Ehrsam, and Brian Armstrong. Zhao is the founder and CEO of Binance, the largest cryptocurrency exchange in the world based on trade volume. Zhao is on this list. He used to flip burgers at McDonald's, but today he is the richest crypto billionaire. A wealth management group called the Devere group surveyed over 700 of their high net worth clients and reported that 68% have invested in Bitcoin or were going to soon. That is impressive once you realize that less than 10% of Americans own Bitcoin, and only 1.5% of the worldwide population own Bitcoin (Redmen, 2020). In a recent article by Jacob Zinkula, he stated that 75% of rich millennials don't think the stock market can generate the return they are looking for and that younger investors are flocking to cryptocurrency, private equity, and real estate (businessinsider.com).

Mark Moss, a nationally syndicated radio host on the iHeart network, explains that Bitcoin is the only digital commodity with no issuers. There is no company, steering committee, or pre-mine where tokens were pre-released to the public. All the other cryptocurrencies, such as Ethereum, had a 70% pre-mine. Bitcoin is a digital commodity and is the only one of the 20,000-plus cryptocurrencies.

## Bitwise 10 Crypto Index

The Bitwise 10 Crypto Index is a market capitalization-weighted index of the 10 largest cryptocurrencies, including Bitcoin, Ethereum, and others. Here are some potential advantages and disadvantages of investing in the Bitwise 10 Crypto Index:

## Advantages:

1. Diversification: The Bitwise 10 Crypto Index exposes investors to a diversified portfolio of cryptocurrencies, which can help mitigate some risks associated with investing in a single cryptocurrency.

2. Professional management: The Bitwise 10 Crypto Index is managed by a team of investment professionals with expertise in cryptocurrency investing. This can provide investors with comfort in knowing that experienced professionals are managing their investments.

3.  Easy access: The Bitwise 10 Crypto Index is available through traditional brokerage accounts, making it easy for investors to gain exposure to the cryptocurrency market without setting up a separate account or wallet.

4.  Regulatory compliance: The Bitwise 10 Crypto Index is regulated by the SEC and operates within a regulated framework. This provides investors with some level of protection and transparency.

## Disadvantages:

1.  Volatility: The cryptocurrency market is notoriously volatile, and investing in the Bitwise 10 Crypto Index can expose investors to significant fluctuations in value.

2.  Limited diversification: The Bitwise 10 Crypto Index only includes the 10 largest cryptocurrencies, which means that investors are still exposed to a relatively small number of assets.

3.  A little history: The Bitwise 10 Crypto Index is a relatively new investment product with limited historical data on its performance. This can make it difficult for investors to assess the risk and rewards of investing in the index.

4.  Fees: The Bitwise 10 Crypto Index charges a management fee, which can affect investors' returns. Additionally, investors may be subject to additional trading fees and expenses when buying and selling the index.

Investing in the Bitwise 10 Crypto Index can expose investors to the cryptocurrency market and a diversified portfolio. However, it's important to carefully consider the potential risks and rewards before investing and to monitor the index's performance closely over time.

One of the biggest and most rapidly expanding crypto asset managers is Bitwise. The company is renowned for managing the biggest cryptocurrency index fund in the world (OTCQX: BITW) and developing solutions for bitcoin, Ethereum, DeFi, and equities indexes specifically targeted at cryptocurrencies. Bitwise collaborates with investing experts and financial consultants to offer top-notch instruction and analysis. Leading institutional investors and asset management executives support Bitwise. The Fund aims to follow an Index made up of the ten most valuable cryptocurrencies, which is then rebalanced, market capitalization-weighted, and vetted for particular risks.

As of April, 2023, the Fund's 5 largest holdings consisted of the following:

| | |
|---|---|
| Bitcoin. | 65.4% |
| Ethereum. | 27.5% |
| Cardano. | 1.6% |
| Polygon. | 1.2% |
| Solana. | 0.9% |

## Grayscale Bitcoin Trust

The Grayscale Bitcoin Trust (GBTC) is a popular investment vehicle that allows investors to gain exposure to Bitcoin without directly buying and holding the cryptocurrency. Here are some potential advantages of investing in the Grayscale Bitcoin Trust:

Easy access: The GBTC is publicly traded on the OTCQX market, which means it can be bought and sold through brokerage accounts like any other stock or security. This makes it easy for investors to gain exposure to Bitcoin without setting up a separate cryptocurrency account or wallet.

Diversification: The GBTC holds Bitcoin as its underlying asset, which exposes investors to the cryptocurrency market. This can be a valuable addition to a diversified investment portfolio.

Regulatory compliance: The GBTC is regulated by the Securities and Exchange Commission (SEC) and the Financial Industry Regulatory Authority (FINRA). This means that it operates within a regulated framework and provides investors with some protection.

Storage and security: The GBTC is held in a secure digital wallet, which helps to mitigate some of the risks associated with holding Bitcoin directly. This can be especially important for new cryptocurrency investors who may not be familiar with the best practices for storing and securing digital assets.

Tax advantages: The GBTC is structured as a grantor trust, which means it can be held in tax-advantaged accounts like IRAs and 401(k)s. This can help investors to reduce their tax liability and maximize their returns.

It's important to note that investing in the GBTC also comes with some potential drawbacks, including high fees, limited liquidity, and a premium over the underlying value of Bitcoin. As with any investment, it's important to do your research and carefully consider the risks and potential rewards before investing.

Grayscale launched the Bitcoin Investment Trust (BIT) to accredited investors. The trust itself owns Bitcoin. An accredited investor can buy shares of the trust in daily private placements. After a 6-month lockup period, the investor can sell their shares in GBTC on the secondary market to retail investors. Grayscale is seeking to convert the trust into an ETF. The thinking is that the disparity between GBTC and the Bitcoin price will collapse as GBTC would become an efficient way to own BTC. One unclear thing, though, is the amount of immediate liquidity current holders of BIT (the underlying trust), who have been locked up, would be seeking. And hence, would the GBTC form of an ETF have an immediate and sharp selloff before it eventually finds parity?

This is something to be aware of, and I would personally study before buying GBTC on the premise that it will collapse to parity if GBTC is approved to convert to a spot BTC ETF.

## Buying Cryptocurrency using an Online App:

Here is a general guide on how to purchase cryptocurrency using an online app:

1.  Choose a Cryptocurrency Exchange: First, select a reputable cryptocurrency exchange that supports the cryptocurrency you want to purchase. Some popular exchanges include Coinbase, Binance, Kraken, Uphold and Gemini.

2.  Create an Account: Once you have selected an exchange, you must create an account. This typically involves providing your name, email address, and other basic personal information. You may also need proof of identity, such as a driver's license or passport.

3.  Verify your Account: After you have created an account,

you will likely need to verify your identity. This may involve submitting additional documentation, such as a selfie with your ID, to confirm your identity.

4. Add Funds: Once your account is verified, you can add funds using a bank transfer or credit card. Some exchanges also support other payment methods like PayPal, but it depends on the exchange you choose.

5. Buy Cryptocurrency: After adding funds to your account, you can purchase the cryptocurrency you want. Select the cryptocurrency you want to purchase, enter the amount you want to spend, and complete the transaction. The cryptocurrency will then be added to your account.

6. Store your Cryptocurrency: After purchasing your cryptocurrency, you must store it in a digital wallet. Most exchanges offer a built-in wallet, but you can also use a separate digital wallet for added security.

That's it! Remember that cryptocurrency markets can be volatile, so it's important to research before investing and only invest what you can afford to lose.

Investopedia describes Coinbase as a trading and investment platform for cryptocurrencies that enables users to buy, sell, and exchange over 100 tradable cryptocurrencies, including Bitcoin, Ethereum, and Dogecoin. With more than 98 million users and $256 billion in assets on its platform, Coinbase is a sizable corporation.

## Here are some of the pros and cons:

Pros

- The Coinbase website and mobile app are easy to use and allow you to quickly buy, sell, and exchange cryptocurrencies.

- Coinbase supports over 100 currencies for trading, which will continue to grow.

- On Coinbase, you can earn interest on eligible balances or earn new currency through Coinbase Earn.

- You can upgrade to Coinbase Pro, an active trading platform with more features and low fees.

**Cons**

- Transaction fees are often expensive on the primary Coinbase platform.

- Coinbase is not known for having a good customer service team.

- Coinbase supports over 100 coins; however, many are not available.

Coinbase's easy-to-use design, educational materials, and solid security measures make it an excellent alternative for anyone contemplating investing in cryptocurrency using the Coinbase app.

1. Download the Coinbase app on your phone from the Apple store.
2. Log in to Coinbase and link a bank account to your Coinbase account.
3. On the upper right-hand side, click Buy / Sell.
4. To choose the asset you want to buy, click the Purchase panel.
5. Input the desired purchase amount in either local money or cryptocurrency.

6. Choose a payment option.

7. Click Purchase Preview to complete your transaction (you can always click the back arrow to make a change).

8. Click Purchase to finish your purchase if the information is accurate.

Choose a one-time purchase and choose how frequently you'd like the transaction to repeat to make it recurring.

## Summary

Bitcoin and other digital currencies distinguish themselves from traditional payment systems through their utilization of blockchain technology, which offers various advantages. Additionally, Bitcoin serves not only as a means of payment but also as an investment and a store of value. However, it is important to note that investing in cryptocurrencies such as Bitcoin has become popular yet comes with inherent risks and may not be suitable for everyone.

# SECTION IV:
# PLANNING FOR YOUR FUTURE

# CHAPTER 15: THE FUTURE OF SOCIAL SECURITY

## PREPARING FOR RETIREMENT IN UNCERTAIN TIMES

> Social Security is not just a retirement program; it is the
> foundation of our nation's social contract"
> — *B. Kennelly*

As my Professor friend Dr. Mike approached his 65th birthday, he couldn't help but feel a sense of excitement and relief. After a long and distinguished career as a Professor, he was ready to retire and spend more time with his family. But retirement also meant navigating the often complicated and confusing world of Social Security benefits.

Fortunately for Mike, he had done his homework and knew exactly what to expect. He had been paying into the Social Security system for over four decades and was eligible for a generous monthly benefit. As he sat down with his financial advisor to go over his options, Mike couldn't help but feel impressed by the efficiency and reliability of the Social Security system. Despite being one of the world's largest and most complex government programs, it operated like a well-oiled machine, ensuring that millions of Americans like Mike received the support they needed in their golden years.

Thanks to his Social Security benefit, Mike was able to enjoy a comfortable retirement, free from the worries and uncertainties that plagued so many of his peers. He traveled the world with his wife, spent time with his grandchildren, and pursued his lifelong passion for history and literature.

But perhaps the most satisfying part of his retirement was knowing that he had played a small role in ensuring the stability and prosperity of future generations. By paying into Social Security throughout his career, he had helped create a safety net that would benefit millions of Americans for decades.

As he sat on his porch, watching the sunset over the mountains, Mike couldn't help but feel a sense of pride and gratitude. Social Security had been there for him when he needed it most, and he knew it would continue to be there for generations of Americans.

## How much money do I need to retire?

Retirement is a time that many of us look forward to, but it can also be a time of uncertainty when it comes to finances. One of the most common questions people ask is how much money they will need to retire comfortably. The answer to this question can vary depending on various factors, but some general guidelines can help you plan for retirement.

First and foremost, it is important to consider your lifestyle and its expenses. If you plan to travel extensively or maintain a high standard of living in retirement, you will likely need a larger nest egg to support those expenses. On the other hand, if you plan to live a more modest lifestyle, you may be able to get by with less.

One commonly used rule of thumb for retirement planning is the "4% rule." This rule suggests that you can withdraw 4% of your retirement savings each year and still have a high probability of not running out of money during your retirement. For example, if you have $1 million in retirement savings, you could withdraw $40,000 annually to support your living expenses. Of course, this is just a guideline, and there are many other factors to consider when planning retirement.

Another factor to consider is your expected retirement length. If you plan to retire at age 65 and live until age 85, you must support your lifestyle for 20 years. On the other hand, if you plan to retire at age 55 and live until age 95, you will need to support your lifestyle for 40 years. The longer your retirement, the more money you need to save to support yourself.

It is also important to consider factors such as inflation, healthcare costs, and taxes when planning for retirement. Inflation can erode the value of your savings over time, healthcare costs can be a significant expense for retirees, and taxes can eat into your retirement income. By considering these factors when planning for retirement, you can better understand how much money you will need to support yourself throughout your retirement years.

In conclusion, there is no one-size-fits-all answer to how much money you need to retire. The amount you need will depend on various factors, including your lifestyle, expected retirement length, and other expenses. However, by considering these factors and working with a financial advisor to create a personalized retirement plan, you can better understand how much money you will need to retire comfortably and enjoy your golden years.

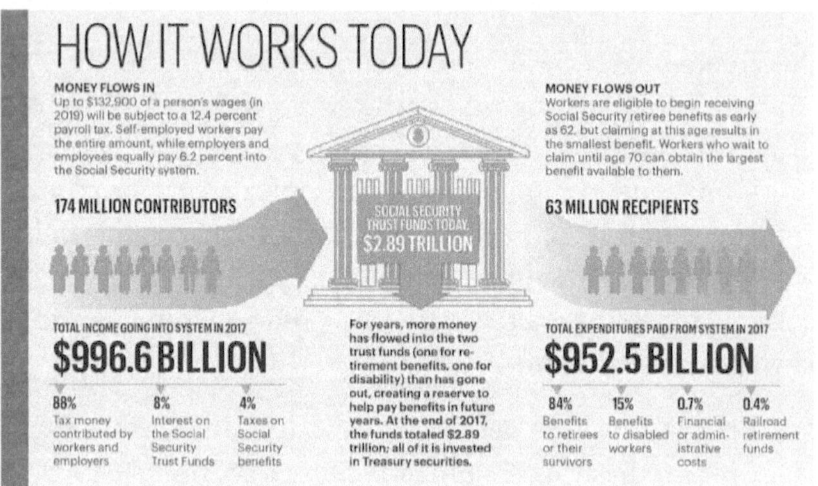


*Figure 17: How Social Security Works*

Based on current projections, Social Security is in a crisis, and without massive intervention, the Social Security program will be insolvent no later than 2033. I do not believe that social security will go away; however, benefits may be reduced, and the average age to apply for social security will increase.

Social Security income is a primary source of income for many retirees today as it is the monthly check they receive from Social Security they live by. Of course, Social Security income was never designed to be a vital component of the average retirement, but only as a supplement. It is the only income stream for 26 percent of American retirees today. That's one out of every four retirees!

As of this writing, the average monthly Social Security benefit for a retired worker is about $1,269, and the highest possible benefit amount paid out is currently $3,350.

## Who qualifies to receive Social Security income?

The list is reasonably comprehensive (including children, the disabled, widows, etc.). Still, for our immediate purposes, you qualify If you are a U.S. taxpayer who has paid FICA taxes for at least ten years (40 quarters) throughout your working life. As contributors to the system, those who qualify to receive a monthly benefit check from the Social Security Administration upon reaching a specific age determined by the federal government.

As of this writing, the minimum age to qualify for benefits is 62. However, determining your monthly benefit is based on your best 35 working years. So, if you worked for 40 years, your five lowest-paying years would be removed from the calculation. Because most people see their earnings rise throughout their life, one common strategy for increasing Social Security income is to ensure that you have 35 high-paying years, which can be used for the calculation. For some, this will mean working longer than they had expected. Another common strategy that can increase your monthly benefits dramatically is to delay applying for Social Security if possible. Although retirees can apply for benefits as early as 62, taking early benefits will reduce your monthly check by 30 percent! Those who can wait until age 70 will get a 32 percent increase in their monthly check. Admittedly, Social Security income may not be as appealing as other income streams discussed in future courses. However, it serves a vital role in most Americans' retirement plans and can make a difference in their standard of living.

My concerns about the Social Security system's financial instability are supported by a wealth of research. Facts are stubborn. Simply disliking them doesn't change them. Therefore, even though I doubt the Social Security system's ability to support itself financially and anticipate significant adjustments in the years to come. For now it makes sense to get the most out of your monthly income and to maximize your monthly benefits as much as possible.

## Social Security Review:

- The most widely used source of retirement

- 24 % of people age 65 and over live in families that depend on Social Security benefits for 90 percent or more of their Income.

- What age can I retire at to collect:

    - Retire at 62 – you will permanently reduce your Income by 20%

    - Retire at 66 – you will receive full benefits

    - If you work at 66 – your benefits will increase by .25 for each month past 66 that you work

    - Born after 1960 – your full retirement age is 67

- If you work after retirement, your social security benefits are reduced if you make over a certain income.

- Social security benefits increase each year with the cost of living

- You will receive 8% per year up to 4 years for each year you postpone receiving your social security.

- Employers and employees pay 6.2 percent of wages up to the taxable maximum of $147,000 (in 2022), while the self-employed pay 12.4 percent.

## When will social security run out of money?

When the last substantial social security law was passed in 1983, benefits were anticipated to be paid in full and on schedule until 2037, when it is anticipated that the trust fund reserves will run out. According to a recent Social Security Trustees report from 2022 (Paul, T, 2022), if Congress doesn't address the social program's financing problems, pensioners will begin receiving a decreased payout in 2034. In other words, even though Social Security will still be around in 2034, seniors will only begin to collect 77% of their entire payment.

According to the Social Security Administration, in 2022, 85 cents of every dollar you paid in Social Security payroll tax went toward the Social Security trust fund, which is responsible for providing monthly benefits to active retirees, their families, and the surviving family members of workers who have passed away. The remaining 15 cents are donated to a trust fund that provides assistance to those who are disabled and their families.

If the trust fund's reserves run out in 2034, current employees will still receive Social Security payments, but if Congress does nothing, future retirees may only receive 78% of their full benefits. Congress must enact legislation to address the Social Security administration's long-term budget crisis to guarantee that workers receive what they were promised.

I've been questioned by numerous students if they can rely on social security and what adjustments will probably keep the current services running. Across partisan and demographic lines, polls have consistently indicated that the American majority strongly supports Social Security. It would be exceedingly difficult to repeal social security because every working generation has made contributions. Citizens understand the importance of Social Security since it provides payments to over 61 million people. Due to the security and stability that Social Security benefits offer to millions of disabled people, retirees, children, and widowed spouses of deceased workers, large majorities of Americans say they don't mind paying taxes on the program.

I think the decisions listed below will need to be made. First, Congress will keep hiking the social security retirement age. Secondly, I think social security payouts could be capped at a lesser amount. Third, the social security taxes will likely increase from 6.2% to some greater percentage.

## Is Social Security keeping up with inflation?

The cost of living adjustment (COLA), which is based on inflation, is intended to assist people in keeping up with the rising cost of necessities such as food, electricity, and housing. Over the past year, prices have surged across the board. The 2023 benefit boost will be the biggest one in 40 years.

The rate of inflation is at its highest point since 1982 as of this writing. For benefits paid in 2022, the Social Security Administration made a cost-of-living adjustment (COLA) of 5.9%, which is lower than the most recent COLA of 8.7% for SSI and Social Security benefits. Starting with the December 2022 benefits, which are due in January 2023, Social Security payouts will increase by 8.7%. Moreover, all Federal SSI payment levels will increase by 8.7% starting with payments received in January 2023.

# CHAPTER 16: FINANCIAL PLANNING FOR THE FUTURE

## NAVIGATING YOUR WAY TO FINANCIAL FREEDOM

"An investment in knowledge pays the best interest.
—Benjamin Franklin

If managing your investments and planning for retirement feels too daunting, then with this new knowledge, you can work with a financial planner. Many investors are unsure where to start or how to maximize their financial resources when planning retirement. This is where financial planners come in. They are experts in helping individuals navigate the complex world of finance and make informed decisions that can lead to a successful retirement.

One of the critical things that financial planners can do to help investors move toward retirement is to create a comprehensive financial plan. This plan considers various factors, including income, expenses, debt, savings, and investments, and helps investors set realistic goals for the future. By working with a financial planner to create a personalized financial plan, investors can better understand their financial situation and make informed decisions about allocating their resources best.

Another important role that financial planners can play is to provide guidance and advice on investment strategies. Many investors are unsure how to invest their money and may be overwhelmed by the many available options. Financial planners can help simplify this process by guiding the different types of investments available and their associated risks and potential rewards. By working with a financial planner to develop an investment strategy, investors can feel more confident in their decisions and have a better chance of achieving their long-term financial goals.

In addition to creating a financial plan and providing guidance on investments, financial planners can help investors navigate the many challenges that can arise when planning for retirement. For example, they can guide strategies for paying off debt, creating a budget, and maximizing social security benefits. They can also help investors to prepare for unexpected events, such as medical emergencies or job loss, by developing contingency plans and building up emergency funds.

Financial planners play a crucial role in helping investors move toward retirement. By providing personalized guidance and advice on financial planning, investment strategies, and retirement planning, they can help investors to feel more confident and empowered in their financial decision-making. With the help of a skilled and experienced financial planner, investors can take control of their financial future and work towards achieving their long-term goals.

# SECTION V:
# PULLING IT ALL TOGETHER

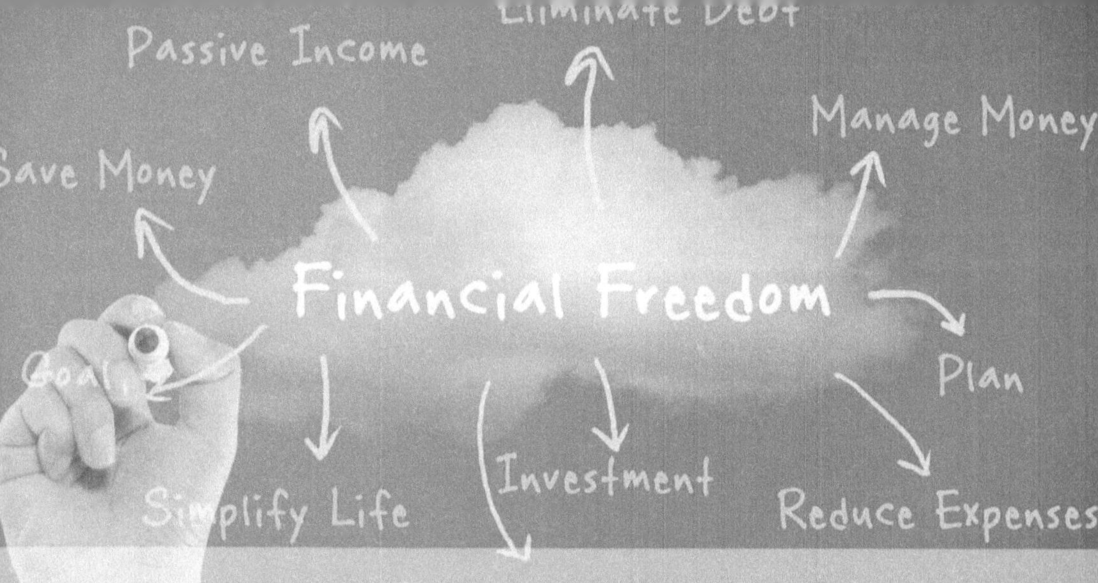


# CHAPTER 17: FINANCIAL FREEDOM STRATEGY

## A STEP-BY-STEP GUIDE TO BUILDING MULTIPLE STREAMS OF INCOME

> "The key to financial freedom and great wealth is a person's ability or skill to convert earned income into passive income and/or portfolio income."
> —*Robert Kiyosaki*

The TIE system is a strategy for achieving financial independence through time, Investments, and Education. By starting early and allowing investments to compound over time, individuals can benefit from the power of compound interest. Making smart investment decisions and building a diversified portfolio can also help to grow wealth and create a secure financial future. Education is crucial, as it allows individuals to stay informed about changes in the market and make informed decisions. By following the TIE system's principles, individuals can build a strong foundation for long-term financial success and achieve their goals.

Financial freedom is the ultimate goal for many people. It means having the ability to live life on your terms without worrying about money. Achieving financial freedom requires discipline, hard work, and a wealth mindset. Here are ten steps that can help you achieve financial freedom.

## Step 1: Have a Wealthy Mindset

The first step to financial freedom is to develop a wealthy mindset. This means having a positive attitude towards money and wealth. Start by believing that you can be financially successful and that wealth is within your reach. Surround yourself with people who have similar mindsets and avoid negative influences.

## Step 2: Keep Building Knowledge and Skill Sets

Continuous learning is the key to success in any field. Keep building your knowledge and skills by reading books, attending seminars, and taking courses. This will help you stay updated with the latest trends and technologies in your industry and give you a competitive edge.

## Step 3: Spend Wisely

To achieve financial freedom, you need to make better financial decisions. Spend wisely by creating a budget, tracking your expenses, and finding ways to reduce unnecessary expenses. Save and invest the money you save.

## Step 4: Pay off Debts

Debt can be a huge obstacle to achieving financial freedom. Make it a priority to pay off all your debts immediately. Start with high-interest debt like credit cards and loans. Once you have paid off all your debts, you will have more money to invest and grow your wealth.

## Step 5: Start a Side Business/Side-Hustle

Starting a side business or side hustle is a great way to earn extra income. Find something you are passionate about and turn it into a profitable venture. This can help diversify your income streams and increase your overall earning potential.

## Step 6: Use Trusted Mentors and Paid Advisors

Surround yourself with people who have achieved financial success. Find a mentor who can guide you on your journey toward financial freedom. Use the services of paid advisors like financial planners, accountants, and lawyers to help you make sound financial decisions.

## Step 7: Invest in the Best Assets

Invest in assets that have a history of producing long-term returns. These include real estate, precious metals, and the stock market. Do your research and invest wisely. Don't put all your eggs in one basket; diversify your investment portfolio.

## Step 8: Build Multiple Streams of Income

Don't rely on just one source of income. Build multiple income streams by investing in different assets and starting side businesses.

This can help weather financial storms and create a more stable financial future.

## Step 9: Compound Money at the Highest Rates Possible and Protect Your Wealth

Compound interest can work wonders for your wealth. Invest in assets that compound at high rates and protect your wealth by diversifying your investment portfolio and using risk management strategies.

## Step 10: Plan Your Social Security and Retirement

Plan for your retirement early on. Start saving for retirement as soon as possible and take advantage of employer-sponsored retirement plans. Learn about Social Security benefits and how to maximize them.

Achieving financial freedom is possible with discipline, hard work, and a wealth mindset. Follow these ten steps and additional tips, and you will be on your way to achieving financial freedom. Remember, it's never too early to start planning your financial future. Start today and reap the benefits for years to come.

## Summary of 10 powerful principles

As you embark on your journey toward investing and success, keep these 10 powerful principles in mind. Let them guide you toward a life of purpose, abundance, and fulfillment.

1. Gain clarity on your "why". When you have a clear sense of purpose and a positive attitude, you can overcome any obstacle that comes your way.

2. Seek out education and mentors. Learning from the experiences and wisdom of others can help you avoid costly mistakes and accelerate your growth.

3. Create multiple streams of income. By diversifying your income sources, you can protect yourself from economic downturns and create more financial stability.

4. Find ways to make passive income seven days a week, even while you sleep. When you have passive income streams working for you, you can enjoy more time freedom and flexibility.

5. Continually raise capital and leverage that money to invest. By using leverage wisely, you can amplify your returns and build wealth faster.

6. Diversify your investments. Spread your risk across different asset classes and industries to minimize the impact of market volatility.

7. Help others along the way. By giving back to your community and helping others achieve their goals, you can experience greater fulfillment and leave a positive legacy.

8. Take calculated risks. Success often requires taking risks, but it's important to make sure that those risks are calculated and based on sound research and analysis. By stepping outside of your comfort zone and taking strategic risks, you can open up new opportunities for growth and success.

9. Embrace failure as a learning opportunity. Failure is not the opposite of success, it is a necessary part of the learning process. By embracing failure as an opportunity to learn and grow, you can become more resilient, adaptive, and successful in all areas of your life.

10. Practice gratitude and positivity. A positive mindset and an attitude of gratitude can help you stay motivated and focused on your goals, even during challenging times. By cultivating a daily gratitude practice and surrounding yourself with positivity, you can attract more abundance and joy into your life.

Remember, these principles are not just ideas to aspire to, but action steps that you can take to transform your life. So, go forth with courage, determination, and a commitment to these principles, and watch as your life takes on new meaning, purpose and abundance.

Congratulations on completing "**Achieving Financial Freedom**" - **Building Wealth Through Passive Income in the New Digital Age of Financial Intelligence**"! You now have a wealth of knowledge and practical strategies at your fingertips that can help you create the life of your dreams. However, knowledge alone is not enough. It's up to you to take action and apply what you've learned to your own life. Whether you're starting from scratch or looking to take your financial journey to the next level, the principles and strategies in this book can help you achieve your goals and build lasting wealth through passive income.

So, I challenge you to take action today. Start by setting clear goals and creating a plan to achieve them. Then, begin implementing the strategies outlined in this book, one step at a time. Remember, building wealth through passive income is not a get-rich-quick scheme, but a long-term journey that requires discipline, persistence, and patience.

But with the right mindset, strategies, and willingness to take action, you can achieve financial freedom and create a life of abundance, purpose, and fulfillment. So, what are you waiting for? Take the first step towards your financial future today and start building your passive income streams.

# Recommended Reading

As a professor, I'm frequently asked by both my students and colleagues for book recommendations. And as an avid walker/jogger and cyclist, I often listen to audiobooks during my morning exercise routine. Therefore, I have compiled a list of my top recommended books, which I hope will be helpful and insightful for anyone seeking literary inspiration and continuous learning on specific investing topics

## Stock Investing:

- "The Intelligent Investor" by Benjamin Graham

- "One Up On Wall Street" by Peter Lynch

- "The Little Book of Common Sense Investing" by John C. Bogle

- "A Random Walk Down Wall Street" by Burton Malkiel

- "The Warren Buffett Way" by Robert G. Hagstrom

## Real Estate Investing:

- "The Millionaire Real Estate Investor" by Gary Keller

- "The Book on Rental Property Investing" by Brandon Turner

- "The ABCs of Real Estate Investing" by Ken McElroy

- "Rich Dad Poor Dad" by Robert Kiyosaki

- "The Complete Guide to Real Estate Finance for Investment

Properties" by Steve Berges

## Cryptocurrency Investing:

- "The Truth About Crypto" by Ric Edelman
- "The Bitcoin Standard" by Saifedean Ammous
- "The Age of Cryptocurrency" by Paul Vigna and Michael J. Casey
- "Cryptoassets" by Chris Burniske and Jack Tatar
- "The Internet of Money" by Andreas Antonopoulos
- "Mastering Bitcoin" by Andreas Antonopoulos

## Entrepreneurship and Side Hustle:

- "The 4-Hour Work Week" by Timothy Ferriss
- "The $100 Startup" by Chris Guillebeau
- "The Lean Startup" by Eric Ries
- "The E-Myth Revisited" by Michael E. Gerber
- "Built to Sell" by John Warrillow
- "Think and Grow Rich" by Napoleon Hill
- "Disciplined Entrepreneurship" by Bill Aulet
- "Business Model Generation" by Alexander Osterwalder and Yves Pigneur

## Gold and Silver Investing:

- "The New Case for Gold" by James Rickards
- "Guide to Investing in Gold and Silver" by Michael Maloney
- "The Silver Manifesto" by David Morgan and Chris Marchese

- "The Gold Watcher" by John Katz and Frank Holmes
- "The ABCs of Gold Investing" by Michael J. Kosares

## Debt Management:

- "The Total Money Makeover" by Dave Ramsey
- "Debt-Free Forever" by Gail Vaz-Oxlade
- "The Simple Path to Wealth" by JL Collins
- "The Richest Man in Babylon" by George S. Clason
- "Your Money or Your Life" by Vicki Robin and Joe Dominguez

## Social Security:

- "The Truth About Retirement Plans and IRAs" by Ric Edelman
- "Get What's Yours: The Secrets to Maxing Out Your Social Security" by Laurence J. Kotlikoff, Philip Moeller, and Paul Solman
- "Social Security Made Simple: Social Security Retirement Benefits and Related Planning Topics Explained in 100 Pages or Less" by Mike Piper
- "The Social Security Claiming Guide" by Jim Blankenship
- "Social Security For Dummies" by Jonathan Peterson

## Personal financial independence

- "The Simple Path to Wealth" by JL Collins. This book provides a practical guide to achieving financial independence through investing in low-cost index funds.
- "Your Money or Your Life" by Vicki Robin and Joe Dominguez. This classic book offers a nine-step program for transforming

your relationship with money and achieving financial independence.

- "The Millionaire Next Door" by Thomas J. Stanley and William D. Danko. This book examines the habits and characteristics of everyday millionaires and offers practical advice for building wealth.

- "Rich Dad Poor Dad" by Robert Kiyosaki. This book challenges conventional thinking about money and offers a new perspective on achieving financial independence through investing and entrepreneurship.

- "The Bogleheads' Guide to Investing" by Taylor Larimore, Mel Lindauer, and Michael LeBoeuf. This book provides a step-by-step guide to investing in low-cost index funds and building a diversified portfolio.

- "The Total Money Makeover" by Dave Ramsey. This book offers a seven-step plan for getting out of debt, building an emergency fund, and investing for the future.

- "The Richest Man in Babylon" by George S. Clason. This book offers timeless personal finance and wealth-building lessons through a series of parables set in ancient Babylon.

- "The Automatic Millionaire" by David Bach. This book provides a simple and actionable plan for achieving financial independence through automated savings and investing.

- "Think and Grow Rich" by Napoleon Hill. This classic book explores the mindset and habits of successful people and offers practical advice for achieving financial independence.

- "The 4-Hour Work Week" by Timothy Ferriss. This book challenges conventional thinking about work and offers a blueprint for achieving financial independence through entrepreneurship and lifestyle design.

## Recommended websites:

Here is a list of websites that should provide you with a wealth of information on the topics covered in Building Wealth through Multiple Streams of Income in the New Digital Age.

1.  Investopedia (www.investopedia.com) - A comprehensive website that provides information on investing, financial news, and analysis of economic trends.

2.  Yahoo! Finance (www.finance.yahoo.com) - A financial news and information website that provides real-time stock quotes, financial reports, and market analysis.

3.  Coinbase (www.coinbase.com) - A platform for buying, selling, and trading cryptocurrencies, including Bitcoin.

4.  Binance (www.binance.com) - Another popular cryptocurrency exchange that offers a range of digital assets for trading.

5.  The Balance (www.thebalance.com) - A website that provides practical advice on personal finance, investing, and money management.

6.  Udemy (www.udemy.com) - An online learning platform that offers courses on a range of financial topics, including investing, cryptocurrency, and financial planning.

7.  Coursera (www.coursera.org) - Another online learning platform that offers courses on finance and investing from top universities and institutions.

8.  The Motley Fool (www.fool.com) - A website that provides

investment advice and analysis for individual investors.

9.  CNBC (www.cnbc.com) - A financial news and information website that covers global markets, investing trends, and economic news.

10. The Wall Street Journal (www.wsj.com) - A news organization that provides in-depth coverage of business and financial news from around the world.

# References

American Payroll Association. (2021). "Getting Paid In America"
Survey. Retrieved from https://www.americanpayroll.org/
docs/default-source/research/2021-getting-paid-in-america-
survey-results.pdf

Board of Governors of the Federal Reserve System. (2021).
Report on the Economic Well-Being of U.S. Households
in 2020. Retrieved from https://www.federalreserve.gov/
publications/2021-economic-well-being-of-us-households-
in-2020-executive-summary.html

Bove, T. Prepare for a 'long and ugly' recession, says Dr. Doom,
the economist who predicted the 2008 crash. Fortune
September. 21, 2022.   https://fortune.com/2022/09/21/long-
ugly-recession-dr-doom-nouriel-roubini/

Charles Schwab. "The power of consistency: Investor insights
on dollar-cost averaging." Charles Schwab & Co., Inc., 2021.
https://www.schwab.com/resource-center/insights/content/
the-power-of-consistency-investor-insights-on-dollar-cost-
averaging.

Clancy, Tom. Without Remorse. (New York: Putnam, 1993), 268.

Dilendorf, R. (2021). Real Estate Investment Funds in a Digital
World. Journal of Taxation & Regulation of Financial
Institutions, 34(3), 21-30.

Einstein, Albert. "The eighth wonder of the world." The
New York Times, April 18, 1983, https://www.nytimes.
com/1983/04/18/business/the-eighth-wonder-of-the-world.
html.

Fidelity. "Investment Management and Guidance - Fidelity."
Fidelity, 2021, https://www.fidelity.com/.

Garcia, Sabrina. "Dr. Doom Nouriel Roubini Says Next
Financial Crisis Will Be 'Worse Than the Global Financial
Crisis'" CNBC, February 23, 2022. https://www.cnbc.
com/2022/02/23/dr-doom-nouriel-roubini-says-next-
financial-crisis-will-be-worse-than-the-global-financial-
crisis.html.

Geske, R. (2021). Real estate investing 101. Journal of Financial
Planning, 34(5), 50-57.

Guglielmetti, C. (2021). Investing in the Stock Market: A Guide
for Beginners. Journal of Financial Planning, 34(6), 62-70.

Henderson, L. (2020). A Beginner's Guide to Starting a
Successful Blog. Journal of Digital Marketing, 32(3), 40-48.

Forbes. Accessed March 19, 2023. https://www.forbes.com/.

https://www.cnbc.com/select/will-social-security-run-out-heres-
what-you-need-to-know/

https://www.brainyquote.com/quotes/ralph_waldo_
emerson_121025.

Kania, B. F., Wronska, D., and Zieba, D. 2017. Introduction to
neural plasticity mechanism. *J. Behav. Brain Sci.* 7:41–8. *doi:*

*10.4236/jbbs.2017.72005*

Klein, E. (2020, October 16). The Pension Benefit Guaranty Corporation is in trouble. Vox. https://www.vox.com/future-perfect/2020/10/16/21519237/pension-benefit-guaranty-corporation-bankruptcy

Lee, S. (2020). Tips for Successful Online Teaching and Tutoring. Journal of Online Learning, 24(1), 16-24.

Morrissey, M. (2019, August 7). Retirement Plans Are Widely Available, But Workers Aren't Using Them. Forbes. https://www.forbes.com/sites/teresaghilarducci/2019/08/07/retirement-plans-are-widely-available-but-workers-arent-using-them/?sh=2b0a8619782b

Nerdwall.com." Accessed March 19, 2023. https://www.nerdwall.com/.

Nesbit, K. (2020). Creating and Selling Online Courses: A Guide for Beginners. Journal of Marketing Education, 42(1), 38-47.

Rabie, A. (2020). E-commerce Success: A Guide to Starting Your Own Online Store. Journal of Small Business Management, 58(4), 71-80.

Romero, M. (2020). Freelance Writing: A Guide to Getting Started. Journal of Writing and Publishing, 13(3), 38-44.

Sireklove, Jennifer. "Diversification in 2021 and beyond: Beyond the basics." Parametric Portfolio Associates, March 18, 2021. https://www.parametricportfolio.com/insights-and-research/diversification-in-2021-and-beyond-beyond-the-basics.

Stokes, Dylan. "Dr. Doom: Stagflationary Bust Looming." Yahoo!

Finance, August 19, 2021. https://finance.yahoo.com/news/ dr-doom-stagflationary-bust-looming-212034134.html.

The Balance." Accessed March 19, 2023. https://www.thebalance. com/.

The Conservative Investor Daily. Accessed March 19, 2023. https://theconservativeinvestordaily.com/.

Tran, T. (2021). Affiliate Marketing: A Guide to Earning Passive Income. Journal of Marketing, 35(2), 16-25.

Vazquez, L. (2021). Social Media Management: A Guide for Small Business Owners. Journal of Small Business Management, 59(1), 58-66.

Williams, Rob. "Should You Convert to a Roth IRA?." Charles Schwab & Co., Inc., March 17, 2021. https://www.schwab. com/resource-center/insights/content/should-you-convert- to-a-roth-ira.

## Quote References:

Barbara Kennelly, former U.S. Representative, "Social Security is not just a retirement program; it is the foundation of our nation's social contract" Kennelly, B. (n.d.). Quotes about Social Security. Social Security Works. https://socialsecurityworks.org/quotes- about-social-security/

Gandhi, Mahatma. "Keep your beliefs pure and good because Your beliefs become your thoughts; Your thoughts become your words; Your words become your actions; Your actions become your habits; Your habits become your values; Your values become your destiny." In The Essential Gandhi: An Anthology of His Writings on His Life,

Work, and Ideas, edited by Louis Fischer, 88. New York: Vintage Books, 2002.

Emerson, Ralph Waldo. "The only person you are destined to become is the person you decide to be." In The Complete Works of Ralph Waldo Emerson, edited by Edward Waldo Emerson, vol. 7, 3-4. Boston: Houghton Mifflin Company, 1903.

Buffett, Warren. "The stock market is a device for transferring money from the impatient to the patient." In The Intelligent Investor: The Definitive Book on Value Investing, by Benjamin Graham, 139-150. New York: Harper Business, 2006.

Poole, John. "You must learn to save first and spend afterwards." In The Richest Man in Babylon, by George S. Clason, 48-59. New York: Penguin Books, 2002.

Buffett, Warren. "In the business world, the rearview mirror is always clearer than the windshield." In The Essays of Warren Buffett: Lessons for Corporate America, by Warren E. Buffett and Lawrence A. Cunningham, 28-40. Lawrence A. Cunningham, 2013.

Colbert, Jean-Baptiste. "The art of taxation consists in so plucking the goose as to obtain the largest possible amount of feathers with the smallest possible amount of hissing." In The Oxford Handbook of the History of Taxation, by Eric M. Zolt and Ajay K. Mehrotra, 34-54. Oxford: Oxford University Press, 2012.

Columbus, Christopher. "Gold is a treasure, and he who possesses it does all he wishes to in this world." In The Diario of Christopher Columbus's First Voyage to America, 1492-1493, edited by Oliver Dunn and James E. Kelley, 98-112. University of Oklahoma Press, 1989.

Emerson, Ralph Waldo. "The only person you are destined to become is the person you decide to be." In The Financial Freedom Formula: A Step by Step Guide to Achieving Financial Independence, by Jacob Smith, 12-13. Chicago: Financial Freedom Press, 2022.

Fisher, Phillip. "The stock market is filled with individuals who know the price of everything, but the value of nothing." In The Financial Freedom Formula: A Step by Step Guide to Achieving Financial Independence, by Jacob Smith, 24-25. Chicago: Financial Freedom Press, 2022.

Rohn, Jim. "Money is usually attracted, not pursued." In The Financial Freedom Formula: A Step by Step Guide to Achieving Financial Independence, by Jacob Smith, 38-39. Chicago: Financial Freedom Press, 2022.

Buffett, Warren. "The more you learn, the more you earn." In The Financial Freedom Formula: A Step by Step Guide to Achieving Financial Independence, by Jacob Smith, 54-55. Chicago: Financial Freedom Press, 2022.

Roosevelt, Franklin D. "Real estate cannot be lost or stolen, nor can it be carried away. Purchased with common sense, paid for in full, and managed with reasonable care, it is about the safest investment in the world." In FDR's Folly: How Roosevelt and His New Deal Prolonged the Great Depression, by Jim Powell, 201-210. New York: Crown Forum, 2003.

Drucker, Peter. "The best way to predict the future is to create it." In The Effective Executive: The Definitive Guide to Getting the Right Things Done, by Peter F. Drucker, 82-94. New York: HarperCollins Publishers, 2002.

Yiddish Proverb. "Interest on debts grows without rain." In The Dictionary of Jewish Proverbs, by Alfred Kolatch, 69. New York: HarperCollins Publishers, 1996.

Jobs, Steve. "Innovation distinguishes between a leader and a follower." In Steve Jobs, by Walter Isaacson, 248-260. New York: Simon & Schuster, 2011.

Brown Jr., H. Jackson. "The best preparation for tomorrow is doing your best today." In Life's Little Instruction Book, edited by H. Jackson Brown Jr., 37-48. Nashville, TN: Thomas Nelson, 1991.

Franklin, Benjamin. "An investment in knowledge pays the best interest." In The Way to Wealth and Other Writings on Finance, by Benjamin Franklin, edited by Janet M. Hartley, 97-104. New York: Barnes & Noble, 2006.

Kiyosaki, Robert. "The richest people in the world look for and build networks; everyone else looks for work." In The Financial Freedom Formula: A Step-by-Step Guide to Achieving Financial Independence, by Jacob Smith, 70-71. Chicago: Financial Freedom Press, 2022.

You can contact me via:

LinkedIn: www.linkedin.com/in/Bobramirezquantumtechnology

Website: www.NewWorldPeopleSpecialists.com

Podcast at YouTube.com/@emergingleadershipbrand

Email address: Ramirez.bob@gmail.com